IN THE PICTURE

LEVEL ONE: CORE

IN THE PICTURE

Level One:
Consolidation Book
Extension Book
Teacher's Book

Details of these Level One books, together with Level Two and beyond, are available from the publishers.

IN THE PICTURE

LEVEL ONE: CORE

Peter Chilver

Stanley Thornes (Publishers) Ltd

First published 1985 by
Stanley Thornes (Publishers) Ltd
Old Station Drive
Leckhampton Road
CHELTENHAM GL53 0DN

British Library Cataloguing in Publication Data

Chilver, Peter
    In the picture.—(Stanley Thornes English Programme)
    Core book 1
    1. English language—Composition and exercises
    I. Title   II. Series
    428.2   PE1112

    ISBN 0 85950 500 6

Typeset by Tech-Set, Gateshead, Tyne & Wear.
Printed and bound in Great Britain by The Bath Press Ltd, Bath

Contents

Acknowledgements

The authors and publishers are grateful to the following for permission to reproduce previously published material:

A D Peters & Co Ltd, for an extract from *Sky In The Pie* by Roger McGough

Brampton Manor School Magazine, for *Paddy*

Collins, for extracts from *The Phantom Tollbooth* by Norman Juster, and *The Lion, The Witch and The Wardrobe* by C S Lewis

David Higham Associates Ltd, for extracts from *To Tea on Sunday* by Leslie Halward, *A Moment in Time* by Richard Hughes, *Collected Poems* by Charles Causley, and *The Secret Brother* by Elizabeth Jennings

George Allen & Unwin, for an extract from *Two Worlds of Childhood* by Urie Bronfenbrenner

Hamish Hamilton, for an illustration accompanying the story *A Happy Prince*, illustrated by Krystna Tursha

Hamlyn Publishers, for a picture from *Thrilling Stories*

Ian Serraillier and Puffin Books, for a poem from *I'll Tell You A Tale*

John Farquharson Ltd, for an extract from *Black Boy* by Richard Wright

Laurence Pollinger Ltd and the Estate of Mrs Frieda Lawrence Ravagli, for *Willy Wet-Leg* by D H Lawrence from *The Complete Poems of D H Lawrence*

Methuen & Co Ltd, for an extract from *Little House in the Big Woods* by Laura Ingalls Wilder

Oxford University Press, for a poem taken from *Out of Bounds* by Jon Stallworthy, and *Frontier Wolf* by Rosemary Sutcliff

Penguin Books Ltd, for extracts from *Ancient Education and Today* by E B Castle, *Soviet Education* by Nigel Grant and *The Tale of Troy* by Roger Lancelyn Green

Peter Lowe, for an extract from *The Evolution and Ecology of the Dinosaurs* by L B Halstead

Radio Times, for an article by Jeremy Cherfas

Syndication International Ltd, for an extract from the *Daily Mirror* (21.7.83)

The Bodley Head, for an extract from *The Boy Who Was Afraid* by Armstrong Perry

The HEARST Corporation, for an adaptation from *Science Digest*

The Society of Authors as the literary representative of the Estate of John Masefield, for the poem *Reynard the Fox*

Vernon Scannell, for his poems *Uncle Albert* and *A Case of Murder*

Virago Press, for an extract from *I Know Why the Caged Bird Sings* by Maya Angelou (1969)
Ward Lock Educational Co Ltd, for an extract from *The Story Teller* by Emma Langland
William Heinemann Ltd, for an extract from *Down River* by Richard Church
Lynn Doody, for *Run For Your Life* (p 11)
Beverley Dowell, for *Paddy* (p 48)
Amanda Drage, for *Things In The Dark* (p 129)
Billy Edwards, for *My Greatest Ambition* (p 50)
Julie Elford, for *Red* (p 10)
David Miller, for *Victim* (p 10)
Amarjit Panesar, for *Bullies in School* (p 98)
Sujitha Ramakrisham, for *A Visit to Kerala* (p 47)
Parvinder Singh, for *My Greatest Adventure* (p 51)
Howard Smith, for *The Day I Was Bullied* and *The Day I Was Caught* (p 100)

We also wish to thank the following who provided photographs and gave permission for reproduction:

BBC Hulton Picture Library (p 111)
Barnaby's (pp 2, 17, 46, 102, 126, 141, 142, 147, and 157 left)
British Museum (Natural History) (p 57)
Bruce Coleman (p 79)
City of Birmingham Museums and Art Gallery (p 45)
Charlton Kings Public Library and Ken Illet (p 24)
Gordon Winter (p 157 bottom right)
Greg Smith (p 16)
Heather Angel (pp 113, 127 and 128)
Jim Meads (pp 78 and 80)
Museo del Prado (p 123)
National Film Development Corporation Ltd (p 157 top right)
Photographic Records (p 137)
Roger Mayne (pp 1 and 103)
The Mansell Collection (p 107)
The Zoological Society of London (p 38)
Universal Pictures, a division of Universal City Studios, Inc, courtesy of MCA Publishing, a division of MCA Inc (p 67)
Welsh Tourist Board (p 115)
World Wildlife Fund (p 58)

Every attempt has been made to contact copyright holders, but we apologise if any have been overlooked.

1 INTRODUCTORY

Milo

There was once a boy named Milo who didn't know what to do with himself — not just sometimes, but always.

When he was in school he longed to be out, and when he was out he longed to be in. On the way he thought about coming home, and coming home he thought about going. Wherever he was he wished he was somewhere else, and when he got there he wondered why he'd bothered. Nothing really interested him — least of all the things that should have.

'It seems to me that almost everything is a waste of time,' he remarked one day as he walked dejectedly home from school. 'I can't see the point in learning to solve useless problems, or subtracting turnips from turnips, or knowing where Ethiopia is, or how to spell February.' And, since no one bothered to explain otherwise, he regarded the process of seeking knowledge as the greatest waste of time of all.

As he and his unhappy thoughts hurried along (for while he was never anxious to be where he was going, he liked to get there as quickly as possible) it seemed a great wonder that the world, which was so large, could sometimes feel so small and empty.

'And worst of all,' he continued sadly, 'there's nothing for me to do, nowhere I'd care to go, and hardly anything worth seeing.' He punctuated this last thought with such a deep sigh that a house sparrow singing near by stopped and rushed home to be with his family.

Without stopping or looking up, he rushed past the buildings and busy shops that lined the street and in a few minutes reached home — dashed through the hall — hopped into the lift — two, three, four, five, six, seven, eight, and off again — opened the door of the flat — rushed into his room — flopped dejectedly into a chair, and grumbled softly, 'Another long afternoon.'

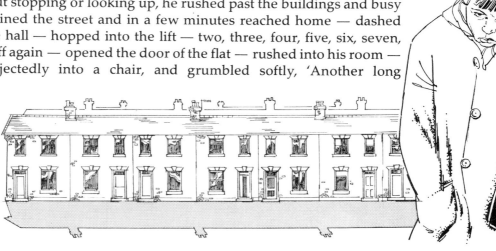

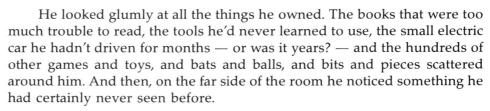

He looked glumly at all the things he owned. The books that were too much trouble to read, the tools he'd never learned to use, the small electric car he hadn't driven for months — or was it years? — and the hundreds of other games and toys, and bats and balls, and bits and pieces scattered around him. And then, on the far side of the room he noticed something he had certainly never seen before.

Who could possibly have left such an enormous package and such a strange one? For, while it was not quite square, it was definitely not round, and for its size it was larger than almost any other big package of smaller dimension that he'd ever seen.

Attached to one side was a bright-blue envelope which said simply: FOR MILO, WHO HAS PLENTY OF TIME.

Of course, if you've ever received a surprise package, you can imagine how puzzled and excited Milo was; and if you've never received one, pay close attention, because some day you might.

'I don't think it's my birthday,' he puzzled, 'and Christmas must be months away, and I haven't been outstandingly good, or even good at all.' (He had to admit this, even to himself.) 'Probably I won't like it anyway, but since I don't know where it came from, I can't possibly send it back.' He thought about it for quite a while and then opened the envelope, but just to be polite.

From *The Phantom Tollbooth* **by Norton Juster**

For discussion

1   **What do you think will happen next?**
2   **Do you think Milo will change in the course of the story?**
3   **How do you think he might change?**

Two Poems

This poem, and the one on page 6, both tell stories. One of them tells the whole story. The other leaves a great deal to the reader's imagination.

The Rescue

The wind is loud,
The wind is blowing,
The waves are big,
The waves are growing.
What's that? What's that?
A dog is crying,
It's in the sea,
A dog is crying.
His or hers
Or yours or mine?
A dog is crying,
A dog is crying.

Is no one there?
A boat is going.
The waves are big,
A man is rowing,
The waves are big,
The waves are growing.
Where's the dog?
It isn't crying.
His or hers
Or yours or mine?
Is it dying?
Is it dying?

The wind is loud,
The wind is blowing,
The waves are big,
The waves are growing.
Where's the boat?
It's upside down.
And where's the dog,
And must it drown?
His or hers
Or yours or mine?
O, must it drown?
O, must it drown?

Where's the man?
He's on the sand,
So tired and wet
He cannot stand.
And where's the dog?
It's in his hand,
He lays it down
Upon the sand.
His or hers
Or yours or mine?
The dog is mine,
The dog is mine!

So tired and wet
And still it lies.
I stroke its head,
It opens its eyes,
It wags its tail,
So tired and wet.
I call its name,
For it's my pet,
Not his or hers
Or yours, but mine —
And up it gets,
And up it gets!

Ian Serraillier

Uncle Albert

When I was almost eight years old
My Uncle Albert came to stay;
He wore a watch-chain made of gold
And sometimes he would let me play
With both the chain and the gleaming watch,
And though at times I might be rough
He never seemed to bother much.
He smelled of shaving-soap and snuff.
To me he was a kind of God,
Immensely wise and strong and kind,
And so I thought it rather odd
When I came home from school to find
Two strangers, menacing and tall,
In the parlour, looking grim
As Albert — suddenly quite small —
Let them rudely hustle him
Out to where a black car stood.
Both Albert and his watch and chain
Disappeared that day for good.
My parents said he'd gone to Spain.

Vernon Scannell

For discussion

1 In *The Rescue,* what has happened to the dog before the story begins?
2 What has happened to Uncle Albert in the second poem before the story begins?
3 What will happen to him next?

The Wooden Horse of Troy

This is one of the most famous of the legends of ancient Greece.

Before you read it, discuss the following:
1   What is a legend?
    Check your definition in a dictionary.
2   What other legends do you know?

After a long war, the Greek army, led by Odysseus, sail away from Troy leaving behind them a great wooden horse. The Trojans think it is a sacrifice to their goddess Athena.

Morning dawned over the windy plain of Troy, and the Trojans looked out towards the great camp of the Greeks which had stood there so long — looked, and rubbed their eyes and looked again.

The camp was a deserted ruin of tumbled stone, and charred huts and palisades. And there were no ships to be seen drawn up on the shore, nor upon the sea.

While they were wondering at this and hardly able to believe their eyes, scouts came hastening to King Priam.

'The Greeks have indeed gone!' they cried. 'The camp lies in ashes; there is not a man, not a ship to be seen. But there stands in the midst of the ruins a great Wooden Horse the like of which we have never seen.'

Then the gates of Troy were flung open and out poured young and old, laughing and shouting in joy that the Greeks were gone at last. King Priam led the way. Everyone stared in amazement at the great Wooden Horse.

At once a great argument broke out among the Trojans as to what should be done with the Horse.

'It is a gift to Athena,' cried one chief, 'so let us take it into Troy and place it in her temple!'

'No, no!' cried another, 'rather let us fling it into the sea!'

The arguments grew fierce: many wished to destroy it, but more to keep it as a memorial of the war — and Priam favoured this course.

At that moment several shepherds appeared, leading between them the wretched figure of a man who was caked from head to foot with mud and filth and dried blood; and his hands were fastened together with fetters of bronze.

'Great King of Troy!' he gasped. 'Save me! Pity me! I am a Greek, I confess it, but no man among you can hate the Greeks as I do — and it is within my power to make Troy safe for ever.'

'Speak,' said Priam briefly. 'Who are you, and what can you tell us?'

'My name is Sinon,' was the answer, 'and I am a cousin of Odysseus — of that most hateful and fiendish among men. Listen to what chanced.

'The time came when the Greeks despaired of conquering Troy: for it was revealed that never could they do so during this invasion. But our Immortal Lady Athena made it known to us that if we returned to Greece and set out afresh, we should conquer Troy. But first we must make this monstrous Horse as an offering to her — and make it so large that it could never be drawn into Troy: for *whatever city contains this Horse can never be conquered.*

'So the Horse was made. But Odysseus said they could not leave Troy without the sacrifice of a noble warrior, and he chose me as the victim.

'Last night they would have sacrificed me: but rendered desperate I broke away, and fled to hide myself in the foul mud of a noisome marsh that drains all Troy. Then the wind rose suddenly and the Greeks sailed away; but whether another was sacrificed instead of me, I cannot say. Only this I can tell you, noble Priam: this Horse is sacred to Athena and — since they have treated me so cruelly I can betray their secrets without incurring the anger of the Immortals — if you take it into Troy, the Greeks will never conquer you.'

Then Priam and the other Trojan lords consulted together. Many of them were still doubtful, but most of them were minded to believe Sinon. So the people were ordered to twine the Horse about with garlands of flowers and drag it across the plain towards the city.

When they reached the gate, the Horse proved too big to enter by it. But the Trojans gaily pulled down a section of the wall, and brought it through in triumph, right to the courtyard of Athena's temple.

Night fell, and the Trojans feasted and revelled in their joy that the Great War was over and the Greeks had gone. At last worn out with excitement and celebration, they fell asleep, leaving few guards by the walls and gates — and few indeed that were sober.

Through the silence the Greek fleet stole back to the beaches, moving through the early night to be there before the moon rose. Then Odysseus (hiding inside the horse with his men) gave the word and they undid the bolt and opened the door beneath the belly of the Wooden Horse. In his eager haste, one of the men sprang out before the ladder was ready, and the fall killed him. But the other heroes climbed down in safety, stole through the silent streets and opened the gates of Troy to the armies of Greece.

Adapted from *The Tale of Troy* **by Roger Lancelyn Green**

For discussion

1 **What are the most interesting legends?**
2 **What do legends have in common? (For example, most of them are about something fantastic such as** *The Golden Fleece.*)

Two Poems and a Story

These two poems and the story that follows were written by pupils.

RED

Red is the colour of a warm fire.
The colour of blood.
Red is the sunrise early in the morning.
The Devil who lives down in Hell.
Red is spicy foods that burn your tongue.
And glittering rubies in a case.
Red is the colour of heat and warmth.
Red is anger.
And temper.
And danger nearby.

Julie, aged 11

THE VICTIM

Mist rising from the ground.
The church bell ringing in the wind.
A creature's howl echoing through the night.
A beast waiting with bated breath.
Its red eyes glowing in the swirling mist.
The grave-digger, spade in hand, his job done.
A low growl, a startled cry.
A flash of fury, the victim's down.
The beast's lips stained with blood.
Silently it moves to find another victim.
No one's safe until the tables are turned
And predator becomes prey.

David, aged 12

RUN FOR YOUR LIFE

It was very early in the morning. I had got up while the cubs were still asleep, to go hunting for breakfast. The sun had only just come up so I had a good chance of pouncing on a sleepy animal before it could get away. I silently stalked through the undergrowth of the woods towards the farm-house where, the day before, I had seen some plump chickens. I came to the base of the hill; the farm was on the other side. At last I reached the top of the hill. I paused looking down on the farm.

A sudden noise made me spin round and then I saw him. He was crouching down behind a small bush some few yards behind me. He was a hunter, one from down in the valley. He had a gun. He was dangerous.

Immediately my thoughts turned to my cubs. Unless I led the hunter away from my burrow the cubs would die. I knew I had to run and run. I must run from the dangerous man with a gun.

I started to run, faster and faster, under bushes and round trees, hoping to lose him, the dangerous man with a gun. On and on I ran trying to lose him, but still he came closer and closer. I was tired now, worn out with all the running.

I spun round and we were face to face. Several shots rang out. I felt an agonising pain in my left leg. I was wounded, but still alive. I sprang up and again started to run. It was painful running now but I kept going. I tried to lose the hunter by crossing back over my trail, hoping that he would lose my scent, but still he came. I was exhausted. I could go no further when I suddenly saw what seemed to be the answer to my prayers, the river.

I jumped in knowing my scent would be lost in the water. The water was icy-cold. Suddenly I saw a dreadful sight, the waterfall! I tried in vain to swim away but the current had caught me. Within seconds I had been swept over the edge.

It was bright and warm the next morning. Everything was quiet except for the early singing of birds and the splashing of the waterfall as it came over the edge. It suddenly dawned upon me, I had survived the waterfall. The icy-cold water had numbed my wound so I could feel no pain. I laid down in the sunshine on a grassy area to the right of the river. I slowly fell asleep, happy that I was safe and that my cubs were safe too. The dangerous man with a gun was nowhere to be seen.

Lynn, aged 12

For discussion

1 Which of the stories in this collection do you think is the best? (It could be the story told by one of the poems.)

2 Which of the stories is the most popular with the whole class? Re-read the story, and talk about what you think makes it so popular.

For improvisation

1 Choose one of the stories that you think would make a good play.

2 Choose one of the characters from the story, and ask someone to imagine that he or she *is* that character. The rest of the class can now interview the character, asking many different questions to build up a picture of the kind of life the character has led and the kind of person he or she is.

3 Choose a scene from one of the stories and act it out, improvising it in your own words.

Suggestions for writing

1 Write a poem or a story about the picture on p. 1. Or bring along some pictures of your own and write about one of them.

2 Write a story about what you think happens to Milo — either before or after the extract you have read.

Suggestions for reading

Joan AIKEN
The Wolves of Willoughby Chase

England has been overrun by wolves. Two young girls fight against their wicked governess, run away, and are threatened by the wolves.

Ted HUGHES
The Iron Man

A clanking iron giant comes to the top of a cliff and topples to the bottom. Then the various parts of the giant get up and start looking for each other.

Katherine PATERSON
Bridge to Terabithia

The new girl, Leslie, invents a secret place called Terabithia. Here she and her friend Jess can imagine all the adventures they wish for. Then something dreadful happens and Jess is brought face to face with something more dreadful than he could ever have imagined.

Jules VERNE
Journey to the Centre of the Earth

An old parchment discloses a secret passage through a volcano to the centre of the earth. Axel and his Uncle Lidenbrock decide that this is too good an opportunity to miss — though a dangerous one.

G. CHANDON
Stories from the Aeneid

The hero's adventures begin with the Fall of Troy. Aeneas wants to continue fighting for Troy, but he is told in a dream that he must escape from the battle and build a new Troy far away across the seas.

Doris GATES
Two Queens of Heaven

A collection of stories of the gods and goddesses of Ancient Greece. Includes the stories of Persephone who is doomed to be the wife of the God of the Underworld, and Pygmalion the sculptor who falls in love with a statue, and Leander who swims the Hellespont for his love, Hero.

Roger Lancelyn GREEN
King Arthur and his Knights of the Round Table

The adventures of the legendary King and his knights, including Sir Gawain's battle with the Green Knight and the story of Arthur's defeat by his enemies.

Barbara Leonie PICARD
The Story of the Pandavas

The Mahabharata is one of the great epics of India. Barbara Leonie Picard retells the principal events of the epic, including the rivalry between the two branches of the Kuru royal family and the disastrous war that this leads to.

Suggestions for reading . . . continued

Collections of short stories:

Isaac ASIMOV and others
2001 and Beyond

Collection of short stories by Isaac Asimov, Ray Bradbury, Arthur C. Clarke and others. All are set in the future, and some in outer space.

Sara and Stephen CORRIN, editors
Stories for Tens and Over

Collection of stories by various authors. Includes P.G. Woodhouse's *The Mixer* in which a dog tells of his own adventures, together with stories by Damon Runyon, James Thurber and Rosemary Sutcliff. A good mixture of stories of very different kinds — humorous, historical, adventurous and fantastic.

Collections of poetry:

Kay WEBB, editor
I Like This Poem

A collection of poems chosen by children for children in aid of The International Year of the Child. Includes *Night Mail, Tarantella, The Highwayman* and *If.*

Ian and Zenka WOODWARD
The Beaver Book of Creepy Verse

Collection of poems about ghosts, ghouls, witches, dark houses, monsters, ogres, phantoms and spells. Includes *The Listeners, Quite in the Dark, Hallowe'en, The Ogre* and *The White Monster.*

2   I KNOW WHAT I LIKE

Titles and Illustrations

1 We often choose to read a story because the title sounds interesting. Look at the titles on the next page, choose the two best ones and invent stories to go with them. Choose two that you have not yet read.

2 The illustration on p. 15 is from a short story. The photograph on p. 16 was taken at a fairground in Germany. The picture on this page was taken at Elswood Pond in Surrey. Make up the outline of a story to go with one of them.

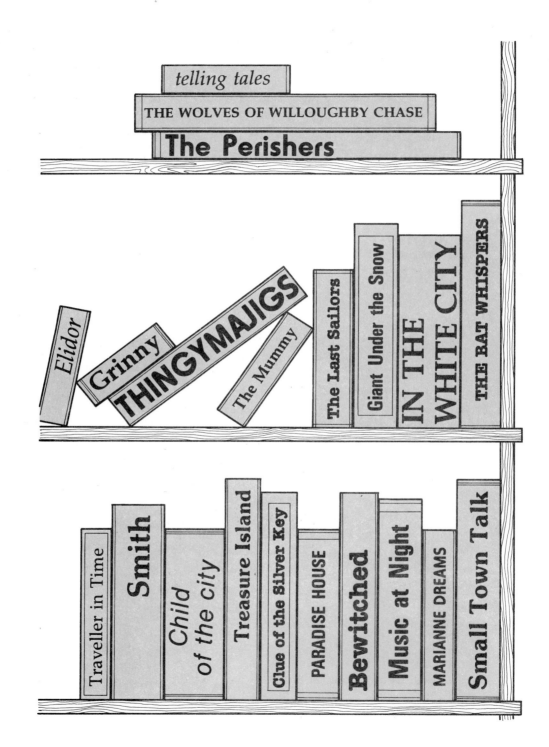

The Synopsis of a Story

A synopsis is a short summary of a story. Newspapers and magazines (such as *Radio Times* and *TV Times*) give synopses of films, for example, so that readers can get an idea of what the films are about and whether they would like to see them. Most novels have a synopsis just inside the cover or on the back of the book.

Here are four synopses, and each one belongs to one of the titles on the opposite page. Can you decide which synopsis goes with which title?

1 Historical fantasy set in the nineteenth century. Two girls fight against their wicked governess and run away. But that is when their troubles and their adventures really begin.

2 An evil creature from outer space comes to stay with an ordinary family, disguised as a long-lost aunt. It is the children who realise something is wrong!

3 Space travellers escape from their ship when it runs out of power, and find themselves in a strange land where the landscape keeps on changing (buildings go up, buildings disappear) but nobody is ever seen. Where is everyone? Science fiction that scatters lots of clues but leaves the reader to put them all together.

4 Steven and Haskmukh are always in trouble with just about everyone — teachers, family, shop-keepers and even the police. But then they decide they want to be detectives and start looking for criminals to catch.

Extracts from Novels

We have looked at the way a title or an illustration or a synopsis can tell you whether you want to read a book. Very often, we also read a little of the book before we make up our minds.

Here are some extracts from different novels. Make a list of four or five different things that you learn about each novel.

1

The sail went first — with a split and a roar. Fragments swept off on the back of the wind. The cords that held the mast hummed like plucked wires. Then with a rending groan the mast cracked. Before Mafatu could leap to cut it clear, it snapped off and disappeared in a churn of black water. The boy clung to the paddle, fighting to keep his canoe from turning broadside. Water swept aboard and out again. Only the buoyancy of tamanu kept the craft afloat. Uri cowered in the bow, half submerged, his howls drowned by the roars of the elements. Mafatu gripped his paddle for very life, an unreasoning terror powering his arms. This sea that he had always feared was rising to claim him, just as it had claimed his mother. How rightly he had feared it! Moana, the Sea God, had been biding his time . . . 'Some day, Mafatu, I will claim you!'

2

The air struck cold, after the August heat outside. George told Andrew to follow him, and John came last, flashing his torch along the floor so that the others could see their footing.

The explosion had enlarged the short stretch of tunnel by cutting away at the floor, and Meaty could get through, this time, without having to strip to the skin, as he had done last year. He leaned over the mouth of the tunnel, closely pressed by the ever-eager Lightning.

'Wait now, while I look,' he said, bringing his arm up and switching on his torch, to examine the effect of the explosion in the great cave.

3   There was a candle by her bedside and she took it up and went softly out of the room. The corridor looked very long and dark, but she was too excited to mind that. She thought she remembered the corners she must turn to find the short corridor with the door covered with tapestry — the one Mrs Medlock had come through the day she lost herself. The sound had come up that passage. So she went on with her dim light, almost feeling her way, her heart beating so loudly that she fancied she could hear it. The far-off faint crying went on and led her. Sometimes it stopped for a moment or so and then began again. Was this the right corner to turn? She stopped and thought. Yes, it was. Down this passage and then to the left, and then up two broad steps, and then to the right again. Yes, there was the tapestry door.

She pushed it open very gently and closed it behind her, and she stood in the corridor and could hear the crying quite plainly.

---

4   It was the sort of house that you never seem to come to the end of, and it was full of unexpected places. The first few doors they tried led only into spare bedrooms, as everyone had expected that they would; but soon they came to a very long room full of pictures and there they found a suit of armour; and after that was a room all hung with green, with a harp in one corner; and then came three steps down and five steps up, and then a kind of little upstairs hall and a door that led out on to a balcony, and then a whole series of rooms that led into each other and were lined with books — most of them very old books and some bigger than a Bible in a church. And shortly after that they looked into a room that was quite empty except for one big wardrobe; the sort that has a looking-glass in the door. There was nothing else except a dead blue-bottle on the window-sill.

'Nothing there!' said Peter, and they all trooped out again — all except Lucy.

---

5   Grinning, Johnny went into the changing-room, pulled off his clothes, and stepped into the shower. Jets of hot water seemed to peel the perspiration off him like a layer of skin. He made a circle with his finger and thumb, and blew soap bubbles over the top of the door, watching them as an upward current of air carried them to the rafters of the gym.

Dad would be pleased at the news that he'd got a place in the team for Saturday. And this time he'd show 'em. He'd really show 'em! No more taking it easy, trying to coast his way through to a win. Whoever was in the opposite corner could expect three ripsnorting rounds, with action up to the final bell.

---

6   As soon as we were all well awake, we fell to discussing the situation, which was serious enough. Not a drop of water was left. We turned the water-bottles upside down, and licked the tops, but it was a failure, they were as dry as a bone. Good, who had charge of the bottle of brandy, got it out and looked at it longingly; but Sir Henry promptly took it away from him, for to drink raw spirit would only have been to precipitate the end.

'If we do not find water we shall die,' he said.

---

7   It was not the first time he had seen fighting, known men killed. You did not serve five years with the Eagles, along the menaced frontiers of the Empire without seeing a certain amount of action. But always, before, there had been somebody else to give the orders . . . Now it was for him and no one else, to give the orders and to make the decisions . . .

For discussion

Re-read the seven extracts and arrange them in order of preference. Which would you most like to read?

What is the best book you have ever read?

All of us have our own preferences for particular books and also for particular kinds of book. Here is a list of books chosen by a class of 12-year-olds, with the name of the person choosing the book in brackets after the title of the book.

The Runaway Summer, by Nina Bawden (Errol)

The Rescuers, author unknown (Matthew)

The Godfather, by Mario Puzo (David)

The Moaning Cave, by Alfred Hitchcock (Vinod)

The Runaway Summer, by Nina Bawden (Amanda)

The Hardy Boys and the Missing Signpost, author unknown (Winston)

Heidi, by Johanna Spuri (Toral)

Pinballs, by S. Boyars (Angela)

The Magician's Nephew, by C.S. Lewis (Maria)

The Mystery of the Magic Circle, by Alfred Hitchcock (Michelle)

Sleeping Car Murders, by A. Christie (Sukhi)

The Exorcist, by William Blatty (Karen)

Tarka the Otter, by H. Williamson (Nicola)

The Spiders, author unknown (Bradley)

The Secret Garden, by F.H. Burnett (Joanne)

Huckleberry Finn, by Mark Twain (Sacha)

King Arthur and the Knights of the Round Table, by Roger Green (Haseeb)

Charlie and the Chocolate Factory, by R. Dahl (Jennifer)

The Mad Dogs, author unknown (Steven)

The Sword in the Stone, by T.H. White (Naeem)

The Great Escape, by P. Brickhill (Barry)

The Omen, author unknown (Nicholas)

James and the Giant Peach, by R. Dahl (Alec)

For discussion

1 Have you read any of the books listed on the previous page?
2 What are your own favourite books? (Fiction or non-fiction.)
3 What seem to be the most popular kinds of story in your own class? (For example, they could be stories about animals or about the future.)

Visit the school library and choose (a) a book of a kind that you know you will enjoy, and (b) a book of a kind that you have not read or enjoyed before.

Punctuation — Writing Sentences

Punctuation is important in helping us to make sense of what we read. Probably the most important mark of punctuation is the full stop, used to show the end of a sentence. As an example, re-read the story of *The Wooden Horse* **on pp. 7–8 and try to imagine it written without any full stops — as one non-stop sentence.**

Here are some *extracts* **from stories written by 11-year-olds. In some cases, they have mixed sentences together. Read the extracts through and rewrite them showing clearly where each sentence begins (with a capital letter) and ends (with a full stop).**

Robert I was all on my own for a very long time. The sea was all around me the only thing I could see was a large bird like a great seagull never in my life had I been so lonely.

Daljit There were a lot of seagulls they kept on flying over me

Mark A storm was building up so I looked for shelter under a tree I thought I heard a noise it could have been a horse that was impossible there are no horses on desert islands

Sarah The ship was sinking fast. I knew that if I stayed on it any longer I would drown I plucked up my courage and jumped overboard

Constantine We were both too scared to do anything if we tried to run away the gang would go for us

John He was the kind of boy who could stand up for himself he had never been scared in his life he could fight his way out of anything.

Jane She wanted to run away but she did not know where to go she wished her friend Jane was here to help her

Ercan We always enjoyed our visits to auntie for the summer holidays little did we know that this holiday was going to be very different.

For improvisation

1 Choose a favourite character from a book, film or TV series. Imagine that you are that character. The rest of the class can now interview you, asking many different questions to build up a picture of the kind of person you are and the life you have led. See how many questions they have to ask before they can work out who you are. (They must *not* ask you your name, or the name of the book or the author.)

2 Choose a favourite book or film. Mime the title for the rest of the class. You can nod or shake your head to any question they ask or statement they make but must say nothing until they give the right title. Count how many questions or statements they have to make before they give the right answer.

Suggestions for writing

1 Make a **chart** for the classroom wall, to show what books are read by the class and who enjoyed reading them.

2 Invent a set of **titles** of books that you would enjoy reading.

3 Invent a set of **synopses** of stories that you would enjoy reading.

4 Write the opening **chapter** of a story that you would yourself like to read — only the opening chapter.

5 Draw an **illustration** for a story that you would like to read. Or collect a picture or pictures from magazines and then write the story.

6 Write two or three **extracts** from a story that you think you would enjoy reading. Ask someone else to write another extract.

Suggestions for reading

Novels with historical settings:

Judith KERR
When Hitler Stole Pink Rabbit

Anna was only 9 years old in 1933 when Hitler came to power in Germany. But she was too busy doing other things to notice the changes that were taking place around her in Berlin and to realise how dangerous it was to be Jewish. Then suddenly her father disappears, and she and her brother are rushed out of Germany by their mother. Then her wanderings and her adventures really begin.

Barbara SMUCKER
Underground to Canada

The young slave Julilly is separated from her mother when she is sold to a new plantation in the Deep South. Her only hope is to escape to Canada. But that is a long way away, and the slave-catchers and their dogs will soon be after her.

Barbara SOFTLY
Place Mill

Story set in England at the time of the Civil Wars of the seventeenth century. Nicholas leaves home to join the Royalist army. Six years later the Royalists have been defeated, Nicholas is on the run, and his life is in danger. He returns home to find that everything has changed. He does not even know if he can trust his own sister, Katharine.

Rosemary SUTCLIFF
Frontier Wolf

Centurion Alexios Aquila is sent as a punishment to take command of a force of frontier scouts in the wild uplands of Northern Britain. The scouts are known as the Frontier Wolves and they have a very bad name. But this is Alexios's chance to prove himself a man.

Stories of children's adventures:

Thea BENNETT (adapted from L.T. Meade)
A Little Silver Trumpet

When Alison's father dies, she and her mother have to move from their cottage by the sea to one room in a grimy tenement block in London. Then her mother is unfairly accused of stealing a £50 note. With the help of her friend Johnnie, Alison sets out to clear her mother's name.

Robert LEESON
Challenge in the Dark

Mike Baxter's first day at a new school marks the start of an unforgettable week. From the moment he comes face to face with the dreaded Steven Taylor and his brother Spotty Sam, Mike is heading for a big challenge. Then his friends help out and that is when his troubles really begin, for Mike finds himself exposed to real danger.

Suggestions for reading . . . *continued*

Walter MACKEN
Flight of the Doves

Finn Dove and his young sister, Derval, are orphans living under the harsh rule of their cruel and selfish Uncle Toby. To escape more beatings, Finn decides to run away and find their Granny O'Flaherty in Galway. With Derval disguised as a boy, the children flee across Ireland, pursued by the police, news reporters and their Uncle Toby.

Michael MORPURGO
Friend or Foe

During the Second World War, two boys are evacuated to a lonely farm on Dartmoor. One night a German bomber crashes nearby, and when the boys go to see the wreckage they find the crew as well — they are still alive and armed.

Stories about animals:

Lavinia DERWENT
Sula

Magnus prefers animals to people, and on Sula, the remote island where he lives, he has many good friends. They include his favourite, Old Whiskers the seal. But then he meets a strange old hermit, and his life is never quite the same again.

Grey OWL
Sajo and her Beaver People

Two Indian children, Sajo and her brother Shapian, adopt two beaver kittens. When their father is forced to trade one of the beavers, they set out in their canoe to look for their lost friend. They have many adventures in the wild woods of Northern Canada before they reach the city where they hope to find their beaver.

Jack LONDON
White Fang

White Fang is the offspring of an Indian wolf-dog and a wolf. A brutal white man called Beauty Smith treats him with cruelty to make him a savage fighter but later he is rescued by a mining engineer who tries to tame him with kindness.

Anne de ROO
Traveller

A true story of the enduring loyalty between a man and a dog. In the 1850s, 16-year-old Tom Farrell arrives in New Zealand to work on a sheep station. While travelling from the coast to the station, he is separated from his guide and is lost miles from anywhere. Then he meets a weak and starving sheepdog.

3 DINOSAURS (1)
Introduction

Tolmodus

Morganucodon

Ichthyostega

Seymouria

1 All about Dinosaurs

Some introductory information

The dinosaurs were reptiles which dominated the Earth for 140 million years. During this time, the world they lived in changed in many ways. The continents drifted apart, the climate altered and plants evolved from simple forms to trees and flowering plants very like those we know today. Dinosaurs adapted to all these many changes with great success. Although in the end they were wiped out by something that we still do not understand, they were nevertheless the most successful and the most enduring creatures this planet has known. Humans have not yet lived for more than a fraction of the time that the dinosaurs lived.

The dinosaurs were extremely big. Even an ordinary, medium-sized dinosaur was twice the size of an elephant. Why were they so big? The reason is this. It is very important for an animal to be able to keep its body temperature at a constant level. If the temperature rises, all the internal processes such as breathing and digestion are speeded up. If the temperature cools, the processes are slowed down and the animal may not be able to function properly. Birds and mammals keep their temperature steady by increasing their metabolic rate, that is, the rate at which their food is burnt to produce energy. The dinosaurs achieved this condition in a different and unique way — they became giants.

As an animal becomes larger, it takes longer to cool down or warm up. Dinosaurs were so big that the temperature inside their bodies must have been amazingly constant, and so all their internal processes could take place at a steady rate without sudden changes. It was this mastery of their own internal temperature that made dinosaurs so successful for so long.

No one has ever seen a living dinosaur. They became extinct more than 64 million years before the first human evolved. Until just over 200 years ago people did not even know that these strange reptiles had ever existed. But we now know, without any doubt at all, that they did exist. In fact we know a very great deal about them and we keep on finding out more.

How do we know about creatures that no one has ever seen?

Adapted from *The Evolution and Ecology of the Dinosaurs* **by L. B. Halstead Published by Peter Lowe 1975**

Multiple Choice Questions

Answer the following questions. Write out the numbers 1 to 10 underneath each other and choose the best answer to each question. Just write (a), (b) or (c). Do *not* write on this page.

1 For how long did dinosaurs live on Earth?
a) For a million years.
b) For ten million years.
c) For 140 million years.

2 Which of these statements is the most accurate?
During the time of the dinosaurs, the Earth changed
a) very little.
b) a great deal.
c) not at all.

3 Which of these statements is not correct?
a) Humans have not yet lived on this planet for as long as the dinosaurs.
b) Humans have not lived on this planet for more than a fraction of the time the dinosaurs lived.
c) Humans have lived on this planet for almost as long as the dinosaurs.

4 Why were the dinosaurs so big?
a) In order to be able to frighten the animals they hunted for food.
b) To keep their body temperature at constant level.
c) Nobody knows why.

5 As an animal becomes larger
   a) it takes longer to cool down or warm up.
   b) it needs much more food.
   c) it becomes stronger.

6 Dinosaurs become extinct
   a) millions of years before humans existed.
   b) just after humans came into existence.
   c) nobody knows.

7 How long ago was it when people first knew of the existence
   of dinosaurs?
   a) Earlier this century.
   b) Some time during the last century.
   c) About three hundred years ago.

8 Which is the correct spelling?
   a) Dinosaur.
   b) Dynosaur.
   c) Dinosore.

9 Which of these statements about the metabolic rate is wrong?
   a) It has an effect on the body's temperature.
   b) It has to do with the body turning food into energy.
   c) It has to do with eating the right food.

10 Which is the wrong spelling?
   a) Temperature.
   b) Creeture.
   c) Reptile.

Using Dictionaries

Dictionaries are helpful for finding out (a) how to spell a word and (b) what a word means.

Words are presented in dictionaries in *alphabetical order.*

In what order would these words appear in a dictionary?
> dinosaur
> prehistoric
> animal
> reptile

In what order would these words appear?
> dinosaur
> dance
> door
> deep

In what order would these appear?
> dinosaur
> dinner
> dine
> ditch

Look again at the passage *All about Dinosaurs.*

1   Make a list of any words in the *first paragraph* that you are not quite sure of. Include words that you *may* know the meaning of, but you are not certain of.

2   Read the rest of the passage. Add any other words that you are not sure of to your list, then arrange them in alphabetical order.

3   Write down what you think each word *probably means.*

4   Now check your answers to question 3 with a dictionary.

Vocabulary

All these words were used in the passage. Write out the numbers 1 to 5 underneath each other and choose the best answer to each question. Just write (a), (b) or (c).

Do *not* use a dictionary and do not use the notes you made on the previous exercise.

1 **Reptiles are**
   a) kinds of dinosaur.
   b) creatures that crawl on short legs.
   c) creatures that reproduce themselves by laying eggs.

2 **Evolved** means
   a) changed.
   b) developed.
   c) changed and developed.

3 **Digestion** means
   a) the process of eating.
   b) tasting food.
   c) the process of turning what we eat into energy.

4 **Unique** means
   a) different.
   b) special.
   c) unlike any other.

5 **Extinct** means
   a) no longer in existence.
   b) excellent.
   c) not very big.

Now check your answers with a dictionary.

2 Dinosaurs — Some new discoveries

It is now 64 million years since dinosaurs vanished from the Earth. But we are still learning new things about them. The fossils of dinosaurs were first discovered not much more than 200 years ago. At first, scientists thought there were only a few different kinds of dinosaur. Now they believe that there were at least 300 different kinds.

One of the latest discoveries is a dinosaur which had a long neck, 40 feet long, like a snake. It weighed 80 tons. It was a herbivore. With its long neck it could have looked into the fifth-floor window of a building. It could also have eaten leaves from the tops of trees.

This is the largest creature ever to have lived on Earth.

But not all dinosaurs were herbivores. For example, the *Torvosaurus* was a carnivore. It was 30 feet long, and weighed about 6 tons. It had very short forelimbs with very strong muscles and it had three very big claws on each forelimb. Its name, *Torvosaurus,* means 'savage lizard'.

In 1978 two American scientists discovered the remains of another kind of dinosaur that was herbivorous and duck-billed. It had as many as 1200 teeth, arranged in layers. With these teeth, it could have chewed even very tough leaves or plants. But the most amazing thing about this new dinosaur was that it seems to have looked after its young in its own nurseries. The scientists found the tiny skeletons of a dozen dinosaur babies inside one nest. Four more baby skeletons were found outside it. These skeletons were too large to have just been hatched and also their teeth were well-worn. They must have had food brought to them in their nest, or they must have found the food just outside it. So it is possible that they were kept there and looked after by older dinosaurs.

These have been named the 'Good Mother' dinosaurs, or *Maiasaura.*

The dinosaurs ruled the Earth for many millions of years. Then all of a sudden, before humans existed, they disappeared. The question is — why? What happened to them?

Adapted from *Science Digest,* **August 1981**

Questions

1 What is the difference between a *herbivore* and a *carnivore?*
2 Why was the 'Good Mother' dinosaur so called?
3 What advantages did its long neck give to the recently discovered dinosaur?
4 What is a fossil?
5 The passage ends with a question. What would be your answer to this question?

NATURE IN DANGER

After listening to the passage, answer the following questions.

Write out the numbers 1 to 10 underneath each other and choose the best answer to each question. Just write (a), (b) or (c).

1   Which plant is now almost extinct?
   a)   Rose.
   b)   Daffodil.
   c)   Ghost orchid.

2   Which of these animals is not mentioned in this passage?
   a)   Rhinoceros.
   b)   Frog.
   c)   Tiger.

3   Which of these animals is now protected?
   a)   Giant panda.
   b)   Frog.
   c)   Woodpecker.

4   Visitors are taken blind-fold to see the
   a)   rhinoceros.
   b)   ghost orchid.
   c)   giant panda.

5   The ivory-billed woodpecker is nearly extinct because
   a)   it is hunted.
   b)   trees are being cut down.
   c)   it is shot for sport.

6   Which of these is *not* a reason why some species are extinct?

a) People have hunted them for sport.

b) People have destroyed the places where they live.

c) They have been destroyed by other animals.

7   The number of species that have been destroyed by people, now equals
a) one hundred.
b) one thousand.
c) one million.

8   This passage could *not* have been taken from a
a) magazine.
b) novel.
c) book about nature.

9   The writer of this passage hopes that a reader will
a) want to hunt animals.
b) want to keep animals in zoos.
c) want to help keep animals alive.

10   Which of these statements is *not* true? The writer thinks

a) nothing can be done to save animals such as the giant panda.

b) everything possible is being done to save animals such as the giant panda and the white rhinoceros.

c) something is being done to save the giant panda.

Punctuation — Writing Sentences

In the previous unit there were exercises on the punctuation of sentences — on the importance of the *full stop* **to show the end of a sentence and the** *capital letter* **to show the beginning of a sentence.**
Here are some extracts from books and articles about dinosaurs. Rewrite them with correct punctuation.

1   Dinosaurs first appeared on the earth a very long time ago they were giant creatures

2   they ruled the earth for more than a million years the early kind of crocodile lived at the same time

3   people have been interested in dinosaurs ever since they first learned about them perhaps this is because they ruled the earth before humans did

4   Perhaps we will never know everything about dinosaurs perhaps too we will always want to know more

5   there have been many films about life in very early times there have been films about people in prehistoric times some of these films have shown people fighting dinosaurs

6   such films are of course telling lies no one has ever seen a dinosaur dinosaurs became extinct long before humans existed

7   Dinosaurs lived long before humans they also lived on the earth for a very long time humans have not yet lived on the earth for so long

8   the earth changed in all sorts of ways while the dinosaurs ruled the earth during that time the dinosaurs also changed

9   if the dinosaurs had not changed they would not have survived so long one of the reasons why they survived was that they were so big

10 people first learned about these strange reptiles over 200 years ago they became extinct more than 64 million years before humans evolved

Using the Library

Look at the illustrations on p. 30.

What do the various creatures illustrated there possibly have in common?

Check your answers in any reference books in the school library.

See what you can find out about these creatures and see what connection they have with dinosaurs.

Suggestions for reading

Don BOLOGNESE
Drawing Dinosaurs

Step by step instructions on how to draw dinosaurs. Very detailed and very informative about the different kinds of dinosaur and about when and how they lived. Excellent black and white illustrations.

Pamela BRISTOW
Prehistoric Animals

Very attractive and well illustrated book, with sections on *The Age of the Dinosaurs, The Ice Ages,* and the *Emergence of Man.* A useful index. Good book to browse through.

John GILBERT
Dinosaurs Discovered

Well illustrated, clearly written, with brief chapters on a range of topics including how dinosaurs lived and what they lived on.

Beverly and Jenny HALSTEAD
A Brontosaur, the Life Story Unearthed

Brontosaurs lived about 150 million years ago. This is a story about how one of them might have lived — what happened when he hatched from the egg, how big he grew to be, the dangers he encountered, how he became leader of the herd, and how eventually another brontosaur took the leadership away from him. Beverly Halstead is an expert on dinosaurs and he explains how he based his story on fossil evidence.

Mel HUNTER
Prehistoric Fishes

Looks at the way different kinds of organism are essential to one another. A short, well illustrated book, and very informative.

David LAMBERT
Dinosaur World, a Piccolo Factbook

Pocket-sized, well illustrated. Topics covered include *Before the Dinosaurs,* the *Dinosaur World,* and *After the Dinosaurs.* Also an excellent section on *Surprising Facts.*

Mark LAMBERT
Prehistoric Life Encyclopaedia

Big, colourful and well illustrated, with sections on the *Birth of Life,* the *Age of Reptiles* and the *Ascent of Man.*

LIFE MAGAZINE (editors)
The Wonders of Life on Earth

Large, well illustrated, specially adapted for young readers. Includes sections on *The Mysteries of Migration, The Evolution of Animal Societies, Strange Partnerships among Animals* and the *Long Chain of Evolution.* Useful index. Good introduction to the ideas of Charles Darwin.

Suggestions for reading . . . continued

Richard MOODY
Just Look at Prehistoric Life
Quite small, well illustrated, with sections on *The Changing Earth, Primitive Beginnings,* and *New Life.* Very helpful list of important words, and a good index.

Andrew SOFTWELL
Animals of the Past
Well illustrated, clearly written. Sections on *The Origins of Life, The Force of Change,* and *The Ribbon of Life.* Useful as an introduction to the subject.

4 MEMORIES

I can remember

A Visit to Kerala

I can still remember my visit to my place of origin, Kerala. It has been four years since that memorable visit, but it still seems to me like yesterday.

Kerala is in South India. Most of the people who live there are Malayalees, like myself. My mother comes from India, but my father comes from Singapore. I was born there, as was my brother, but I had to come to England at the age of three. I went back there at the age of eleven.

For an eleven-year-old, the plane trip was a big adventure, let alone visiting one's place of birth after eight years. On the way to the airport I was filled with excitement, but when I started to say goodbye to the friends who had come to see me off I felt really sad. I was being stupid. I'd only be away six weeks. But six weeks to me then seemed like a million years . . .

My first glimpse of India was breathtaking. The sun was shining, the sky a clear blue with not a single cloud in sight. The small Trivandrum Airport was surrounded by tall palm trees. As I got out of the plane, I saw that the entrance of the airport was surrounded by people waiting for their friends and relatives. I searched in amongst the crowd for the faces of my uncle Manu, the youngest of my uncles, and my grandad. But none of the faces I saw fitted in with the image I had conjured up in my mind. 'There they are,' my mum said, pointing to a young man who was walking towards us and an old man with a cane walking behind him. 'Sathana Maul, it is nice to see you,' said my grandad, hugging her, 'and these are my three grandchildren!'

He picked up my little sister and kissed her on the cheek. I felt stupid. I didn't know what to do. Uncle Manu took hold of mine and Biju's hand and led us through the crowds, leaving my parents and grandad to follow.

I don't remember much of the ride to my village, Kaddakavar, partly because I was tired and also the excitement was too much for me. I fell asleep against my mum's arm. But I was woken up before we reached my grandma's house. In front of the house was a sort of miniature meadow with palm trees. You had to walk through the meadow before you reached the house. As I neared the house, I couldn't see much of it except the roof. The house was surrounded by a wall and in the middle of the wall was a big wooden gate. As I neared the gate it opened, and a small lady appeared. She was dressed in a white sari.

She rushed up to us, her old face wrinkled into a smile. Her eyes were moist as she hugged my brother, sister and myself. She was, of course, my grandmother . . .

As the days went on, I got over my homesickness for England. We visited many places, for example Kovalam Beach, a lovely beach on the outskirts of Trivandrum, the capital of Kerala. The sand was black and the sea was blue. We visited Thirajpathy Temple. This is situated on the top of a hill. On the sides of the hill, rubber trees grow. The temple is huge, as tall as the skyscrapers in New York. We went to see the sun rise at Kanjakumari. As the sun slowly rises above the horizon, the sky turns a brilliant orange which sets the whole sea aflame.

Sujitha, aged 14

For discussion

1　**Have you ever made a specially memorable visit any-where?**
2　**What different kinds of thing make such occasions memorable?**

SNIFF
SNIFF

Paddy

I can remember my old dog Paddy. He's dead now, unfortunately, but he was terrible when he was alive. It was me who found him, or rather him who found me! He followed me, but when I tried to stroke him he growled and bared his teeth. He must have wanted my attention, but was afraid I might hurt him. He slept outside my house one night, then my mother took him to the police station and reported him 'a stray'. We really did miss him, so she went and got him back and said that we'd keep him. He wasn't the best of lookers, dog-wise, in fact I haven't seen much worse. The police described him as three foot long, one foot high! He had black and white patches all over his body, his coat was long and scruffy and he never looked clean. He wasn't any particular type of breed or cross-breed; he was as long as a dachshund, as high as a spaniel; he had a head like a sheepdog, a body like a corgi and a tail like a German shepherd.

He was a born fighter, old Paddy was! My two cats began to live upstairs; they kept well away from him. He had a vicious personality. He used to growl at anything and everything. I even watched him growl at car wheels and trees. He would growl at old ladies and men on walking sticks, and he couldn't resist a fight. No matter what breed or size the dog was he would fight it. My neighbour had an Alsatian and Paddy always jumped the garden fence and barked through the window at it, and when it came out he used to fight like mad. He used to come out of fights badly, but the other dog was a lot worse off. On occasions Paddy tore through other dogs' ears with his teeth; he bit hard into their legs until the bone showed and bit straight through the sides of their mouths. I can remember him always coming home from his walk covered in thick dried-on blood, and either my mother or I had to sit with him bathing his wounds. But as much as he suffered, he just wouldn't give up fighting. He must have been the equivalent to Mohammed Ali!

The funny thing about him was, to my parents and me he was the most loving thing on four legs. When I called him, he couldn't get close enough to me. But my brother and cousins were really cruel to him. They used to hit him with sticks. One day they tied him up in an old shed and then they threw stones and sticks at him. Another day they took him out and as he was running around they jumped on a bus and left him miles from home. My mother was furious. She drove around the streets at two and three in the morning; she had no luck in finding him.

But sure enough! Who should turn up at our front door next morning? You've guessed, Paddy! He looked worn out, and his feet were sore. He continued his fighting and my brother kept tormenting him. Eventually my mother said it would be best for him to be 'put down'. I disagreed furiously, but one day I came home from school and found him gone. I thought he was out on one of his walks, but when my mum told me I went mad! I couldn't stop crying. I phoned the vets to see if he was still alive but he wasn't. I still miss him now, but I realise it was the best thing for him. Now he has no one to torment him and he can't continue fighting — and even I know that he led a terrible life. I wonder what his life was like before I found him?

Beverly, aged 14

For discussion

1 **Should Paddy have been put down?**
2 **What do you think Paddy's life was like before the writer found him?**
3 **Have you ever had a similar experience with an animal?**

My Greatest Ambition

My greatest ambition is to be a bass guitarist for a group when I leave school. A few friends and I have already started a small group and started practising a few weeks ago. We had to stop practising because Jimmy Taylor's amplifier stopped working. I am the bass guitarist, Jimmy is lead guitarist, and David Head is drummer. We chose David to be drummer because he likes to sit down and rest all the time.

We have got our musical side sorted out and now we need a singer. We can't play anywhere at the moment because we are not old enough, but we are hoping to play in pubs and things later. We could easily get in pubs to do backups for Tone Deaf, of which Dave's brother, Rob, is bass guitarist. At first it was hard to find a name for our group, but we ended up with the name Target. Jimmy Taylor thought of the name and I thought of the design that we painted on the drum skin. It is a target with 'Target' written across the bull's eye.

For the past few weeks we have practised in each other's houses, but now we have found a place to play. With any luck, I am moving in the middle of June to a new house just past Wanstead. It is a corner house with a garage and we are going to practise in the garage. We will keep the equipment in the garage and my dad will pick up Jimmy and Dave on his way home from work, because my dad's workshop and office is down the same road where I live now. So when he comes home he can bring them with him. My greatest ambition is not only to be bass guitarist, but for the group to be well-known when we get older.

Our group may be practising again by the start or middle of June. At first, Kevin Harvey was going to be singer; that was when we used to hang about Petticoat Lane and Portobello Road. But when we were just about to start, there were continual rows between him and us because he was picking on Dave, so we chucked him out.

If we don't find a singer soon, either Jim or I will have to choose which one of us will be singer. Of course we may not make it anywhere when we get older, but we are getting enjoyment just from practising.

If we did make it to producing records, we don't want to make too much money because if you get too much money you get greedy and this is mainly why groups split up. Last week, Dave got a few lessons from Jimmy's dad after he came back from the pub. Jimmy's dad wasn't drunk but he was a lot happier than usual.

Jim and I get lessons from Robert sometimes who has played in pubs and clubs. We are glad to have Dave's brother teaching us things, because he's like a manager really and helps us when he can.

Billy, aged 12

For discussion

What are the most common and most uncommon ambitions in your class?

A group of pupils talked about the most adventurous things that had ever happened to them. Some of them invented stories to see if the others believed them. Here is one of the stories they told. Do you think it is true or false?

My Greatest Adventure

Once I went swimming down in Cornwall with my friend Rajinder. We were on holiday with his parents. I love swimming, but Rajinder was only just learning and he wasn't really very good at it. I was teaching him. I think it will be a long time before I try to teach anybody to swim again. At first, we did quite well. Rajinder could swim a little, then a little bit more, and then he seemed rather good at it. We used to go swimming early in the morning, and we had found a lovely bay where nobody else ever seemed to go.

This particular morning, we got down to the bay as soon as we could, there was no one around and the sun was shining. I swam out twenty yards or so, and Rajinder swam after me. We swam on happily, not caring where we were going. Suddenly Rajinder called out to me, 'I'm out of breath! I'm drowning!' I called back to him, 'Not to worry! You'll be okay! Don't worry!' But I could see that we had swum out a long way from the beach, and there was nobody in sight to help us. Rajinder was really scared now, calling out, 'I'm drowning! I'm drowning!' What was I to do? I'd never even tried to save anyone's life before and I was beginning to get really scared, just like Rajinder. I could keep myself from drowning, but what about him?

Parvinder, aged 11

For discussion

1 Working in groups, tell stories of your own adventures. Try and decide whether the stories are true or false.

2 Choose one of the stories to tell to (and test) the whole class.

Capital Letters

Capital letters are used in writing to show
a) the beginning of a sentence. For example:
  They reached the end of the journey.
b) the names of people or places or things. For example:
  Jack met Joan in Italy.
  They met on the first Monday in July.
Also, the word 'I' is always written as a capital letter even if it is not at the beginning of the sentence. For example:
Joan and I went to Spain for our holiday.

Re-read the first four paragraphs of *A Visit to Kerala* on p. 47 and count the number of capital letters used. Then check why they are used. How many times are they used
a) to show the beginning of a sentence?
b) to show the names of people, places or things?
c) to show it is 'I'?

The following sentences **contain mistakes in punctuation. Rewrite them correctly. Do not alter the words.**

1   i was born there, as was my brother, but i had to come to England at the age of three.

2   My first glimpse of india was very exciting.

3   Uncle Manu took hold of my hand and riju's hand.

4   the house was surrounded by a wall.

5   uncle Manu took hold of my hand and Riju's hand.

6   The house was surrounded by a wall

7   when i tried to stroke him, he growled and bared his teeth.

8   I can remember my old dog paddy

9   we lost him in wanstead.

10   he could fight like mohammed ali.

11   jim and i gave lessons to dave.

12   we are glad to have dave's brother teaching us

13   my best adventure was when i was on holiday

14   i went to cornwall with my family.

15   The weather was bad all the time i was there

For improvisation

1   **Choose one of the stories you have read in this unit or one of the stories you have told each other.**

Choose your favourite character from that story — it could, for example, be Paddy.

The rest of the class can now interview you, asking questions about you, about your life, about your likes and dislikes — as if you are the character you have chosen.

2 Choose a scene from one of the stories (your own, or someone else's, or from one of the stories in this unit) and improvise it, that is, act it out in your own words.

For example, you could improvise the scene where Sujitha returns to school and tells her friends about the visit to Kerala, or the scene where Beverly is told by her parents that Paddy has been 'put down'.

3 Working in small groups improvise a story that could be (and perhaps is) something that has really happened to you. Then see if the rest of the class can spot whether it is true or not.

Suggestions for writing

1 Write briefly about all or some of the following.
    A memorable visit.
    A great ambition.
    A great adventure.
    A friend.
    A member of your family.
    An animal.
Perhaps add some photographs and other illustrations and suggest a title for the collection.

2 Interview a friend or relative and get them talking about themselves. Work out beforehand the kinds of thing you want them to talk about. Write a report.

3 Make a collection of some of the adventures told by people in the class. Send them to another class to see how many they can work out correctly. Which are true or false?

4 Write a story suggested by the picture on p. 45 or 46. Or bring some old photographs from home and write a story or stories based upon them.

5 Write a play based on one of your improvisations.

Suggestions for reading

There are many excellent books devoted to people's memories and recollections. Here is a small cross-section:

Winifred FOLEY
A Child in the Forest

Winifred Foley's father was a miner and she was brought up in a village in the Forest of Dean. Her life was one of poverty but also of love and happiness. Ideal book to browse through, with some excellent chapters on *Granny and Grancher* and on *The Doll.*

Helen FORRESTER
Twopence to Cross the Mersey

The story of Helen Forrester's poverty-stricken childhood in Liverpool in the 1930s, and later, in the South of England. Sad and also amusing.

Anne FRANK
Diary of Anne Frank

A girl's diary of her life in hiding in Holland in the Second World War, trying to avoid capture by the Gestapo, and death, as a Jew, in a concentration camp.

Thor HEYERDAHL
The Kon-Tiki Expedition

The story of six young men who sail across the Pacific on a balsa-wood raft, told by one of the young men. Full of adventure and excitement.

Sheila HOCKEN
Emma and I

The story of a blind girl who gains independence through her guide dog and then regains her sight through the work of a remarkable surgeon. The story is stolen, though, by Emma the guide dog.

A.S. JASPER
A Hoxton Childhood
Memories of growing up in London's East End at the time of the First World War. It is the story of a London that no longer exists, but the life described existed in all industrial cities at that time.

OUR LIVES
A collection of young people's autobiographies published by the English Centre of the Inner London Education Authority.

Suggestions for reading . . . continued

Emanuel LITVINOFF
Journey Through a Small Planet

Emanuel Litvinoff was born in Whitechapel in East London and worked in various occupations, including tailoring and cabinet making, in the time just before the Second World War. Ideal book to browse through and with some excellent chapters on his *Mother*, his *Uncle Solly*, and *The Geography Lesson*.

Alan MARSHALL
I Can Jump Puddles

Alan Marshall was crippled as a small boy by the disease of poliomyelitis. His world was the Australian countryside early this century — a world of rough riders, bushmen, farmers and tellers of tall stories. Despite his handicap, Alan learned to climb, fight, swim, ride and laugh.

Ezekiel MPHAHLELE
Down Second Avenue

The true story of a black child's life in South Africa. Ezekiel was brought up in the country as a tribal herd boy and was taken to live in a city slum at the age of 13. There he came up against the harsh realities of racial prejudice and discrimination. Many excellent chapters, including *Backward Child, Fight with Abdool* and *St. Peter's School*.

Alan PARKER
Puddles in the Lane

Novel about children evacuated from London in the Second World War. Not strictly a memoir or autobiography but obviously based on rich personal experience. The novel has an interesting glossary at the end of the book, of words that were much used by children of the time.

Antonia WHITE
Frost in May

Again a novel rather than, strictly speaking, a memoir, but again it is obviously based on rich personal experience. The story of a young girl's life in a Convent School just before the First World War.

5 DINOSAURS (2)
and other species

Cloze Test

MORE ABOUT DINOSAURS

This passage picks up some of the points made about dinosaurs in Unit 3. Read the passage carefully. Then choose *one* word, and *only one* word for each space. Write down the numbers 1 to 10 underneath each other in your notebooks, and then write down the best word against each number.

It was not very long ago that scientists discovered that dinosaurs had once existed. Ever since then, people have wanted to — (1) — more about them. In many ways, dinosaurs are the most — (2) — creatures ever to have lived on the earth. And the more we — (3) — about them, the more we want to know.

Some dinosaurs were — (4) —, some were carnivores. All of them were big, and many of them were — (5) — big. One kind of dinosaur was the biggest creature ever to have — (6) — . It was so big it could have looked through a fifth-floor window.

Dinosaurs ruled the — (7) — for roughly 140 million years. They disappeared long before humans came into existence, and humans have so far existed for less than half a — (8) — years. So humans have a long way to go before they do — (9) — than the dinosaurs. But the most interesting question of all, is why did they disappear? What —(10) — to them?

Re-read the whole passage carefully before finally deciding on your answers.

What happened to the Dinosaurs?

Sixty-four million years ago, life on Earth suddenly changed. In the shallow waters of the oceans, vast numbers of creatures died. Something like three-quarters of all known species vanished in an event that has often been described as catastrophic or cataclysmic. On land, too, there was extinction on a massive scale, most notably among the animals whose rule the catastrophe brought to a close: the Age of the Dinosaurs came to an end at the same time, 64 million years ago.

Why did so many species die out at once?

The end of the dinosaurs is an important event, because the dinosaurs left the stage clear for the mammals to take over and eventually humans took over from the mammals. So what caused them to come to an end?

There have been many different theories. Some have argued that the growth of mountains caused a change in the wind-flow and so caused a change in climate, and that the dinosaurs could not cope with this change. Another popular theory is that plants suddenly started to produce a poisonous effect on the dinosaurs and killed them off.

There is another theory that dinosaurs were simply too stupid and were killed off by more intelligent forms of life. But this is itself a rather foolish idea, for in many respects the dinosaurs were very well adapted to the world they lived in, and very adaptable. There is also the theory that death was caused by a huge increase in cosmic radiation, which followed from the explosion of a nearby star.

These are all interesting theories, but they all suffer from the same weakness: there has never been any real evidence to support or prove any of them.

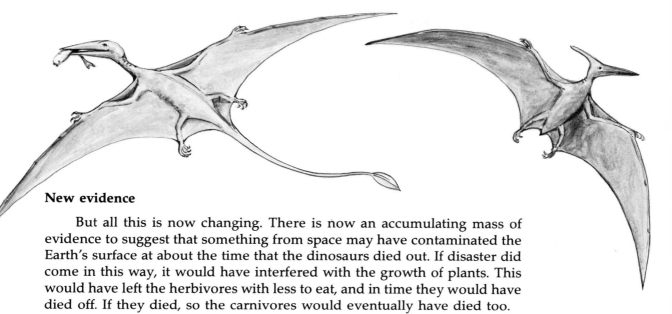

New evidence

But all this is now changing. There is now an accumulating mass of evidence to suggest that something from space may have contaminated the Earth's surface at about the time that the dinosaurs died out. If disaster did come in this way, it would have interfered with the growth of plants. This would have left the herbivores with less to eat, and in time they would have died off. If they died, so the carnivores would eventually have died too.

The only trouble is that the rest of the evidence does not support this theory. Fossils found in Alberta and Montana, for instance, suggest that many of the plants which the dinosaurs lived on, died out *after* the extinction of the dinosaurs — quite a long time after!

So although we have lots of interesting and clever theories, it is fair to say that we still do not really know what made the dinosaurs disappear. What went wrong for them?

Adapted from an article in the *Radio Times* **by Jeremy Cherfas**
14th November 1981 (published by the BBC)

For discussion

1 Which theory about the disappearance of the dinosaurs does this writer think foolish?
2 Why does the writer think that the death of the herbivores would lead to the death of the carnivores?
3 Why does the writer think that something from space did *not* kill off the plants?
4 Does the writer have any theory of his own which explains why the dinosaurs disappeared?
5 What do these words mean in the passage?
   species (1st paragraph)
   contaminated (6th paragraph)
   fossils (7th paragraph)

Dinosaurs — a review

This section of the work aims to bring together all the various things you have talked and read about on the subject of dinosaurs.

To answer these questions you should refer to the three passages you have read in this unit and also pp. 31 and 36 in Unit 3.

1 Roughly how long ago did the dinosaurs disappear from the Earth?
2 For how long did dinosaurs rule the Earth?
3 How recently did people first learn of the existence of dinosaurs?
4 How many different kinds of dinosaur were there?
5 Name two different kinds of dinosaur, and say what was special about each one.
6 Would it have made any difference to us if the dinosaurs had not disappeared?
7 Why was it so useful for dinosaurs to be so big?
8 Explain what a fossil is.
9 Explain what a theory is.
10 How many theories can you think of to explain why the dinosaurs disappeared?
    Which is the best theory, and why?
11 What questions do you still wish to ask about dinosaurs?
12 A *glossary* is a list of important words connected with a topic or subject. Make a list of all the important words to do with dinosaurs from these three passages. Arrange them in alphabetical order, and give their meaning.
13 Look at the illustrations on p. 58. What are these animals? What do they have in common with each other?
14 What do the animals on p. 58 have in common with the animals on p. 30?

Using the Library

Choose a topic on which you would like to do some research. If you wish, choose to do some more work on dinosaurs. Or choose a topic of your own.

First, write a short account of what you know about the topic already.

Then, make a short list of the questions you wish to find answers to.

Then, visit the library and browse through any books on the topic.

Make a note of the title of each book, and underneath the title note down the following information:

> Author.
> Date of publication.
> Does it have a list of contents?
> Does it have an index?
> Does it have a glossary?
> Does it have any photographs?
> Does it have any other illustrations?
> Does it answer any of my questions?
> How does it answer them?

Choose the best book on your topic and borrow it from the library. Now make a note as you look through it again, of any new ideas and information that it gives you.

Finally, prepare a report on your topic for use by other pupils who do not necessarily know anything about it. Make a report that will interest them and get them thinking. It could be like a work-sheet. It could include

> a collection of interesting items of information which begin with 'Did you know?'
>
> a quiz (a set of questions with answers).
>
> a bibliography (a short list of good books on the subject).
>
> a set of questions which you yourself do not know the answer to.
>
> a picture or some other illustration.
>
> a glossary (a list of important words on the subject, in alphabetical order, with their meanings).

Suggestions for reading

Most of the books recommended here are more advanced than those recommended at the end of Unit 3. Most of them move the subject on from the dinosaurs to wider questions of the evolution of human life.

Charles DARWIN
The Voyage of the Beagle

Darwin's own account of the journey that led him to rethink how life developed on Earth. Some recent editions are beautifully illustrated.

Michael DAY
Fossil Man

Michael Day traces the evolution of human life from the early primates, through ape men to the early and later humans. Explains how fossils are dated and how they are studied in laboratories. Well illustrated, very informative, and with a list of other books to read and of places to visit.

Mel HUNTER
Prehistoric Plants

Explores the evolution of plant life and shows the importance of plants in life on Earth today. Well illustrated.

Arthur Conan DOYLE
The Lost World

Fantastic adventure story in which a news reporter is involved in an expedition into the depths of the Amazon jungle. Here he finds a lost world inhabited by dinosaurs and ape-men. Nothing can save him or his friends — it seems — from a horrible death!

Kathleen FIDLER
The Boy with the Bronze Axe

An adventure story set in a Stone Age village. A strange boy suddenly arrives with an axe made from a substance he calls bronze. The boy makes friends and enemies — for there are those who welcome his new ideas and those who are afraid of them. An interesting novel that makes a real attempt to capture the mood and feel of a prehistoric time.

Roger HAMILTON
Fossils and Fossil Collecting

Well illustrated, full of detail and clearly written. Includes information on how to collect and prepare fossils and how to place them in the correct position in the geological time-scale. Useful glossary and index.

Suggestions for reading . . . continued

Anne MILLARD
Early Man

A small but well illustrated and clearly written book. Includes sections on *Discovering Early Man, Family Man* and *The Rise of Modern Man.* Useful index.

Richard MOODY
Prehistoric World

Large, lavishly illustrated account of the 3400 million years before modern man. Sections include *The Birth of the Solar System, The Age of Fishes* and *The Age of the First Reptiles.*

Eckehard MUNCK
Biology of the Future

Moves the subject of dinosaurs on from the study of the past to the study of the future — one chapter is entitled, *Where To, Adam?* There are also sections on stress and worry and the different ways in which people today have to cope with these. An interesting book to browse through, and well illustrated.

PURNELL'S *Prehistoric Atlas*

An illustrated guide to the origins of life on Earth. Detailed and informative, and well illustrated. There are sections on all the main geological eras and there is also a useful index. Very good book for tracking down various items of information.

6 BULLYING (1)

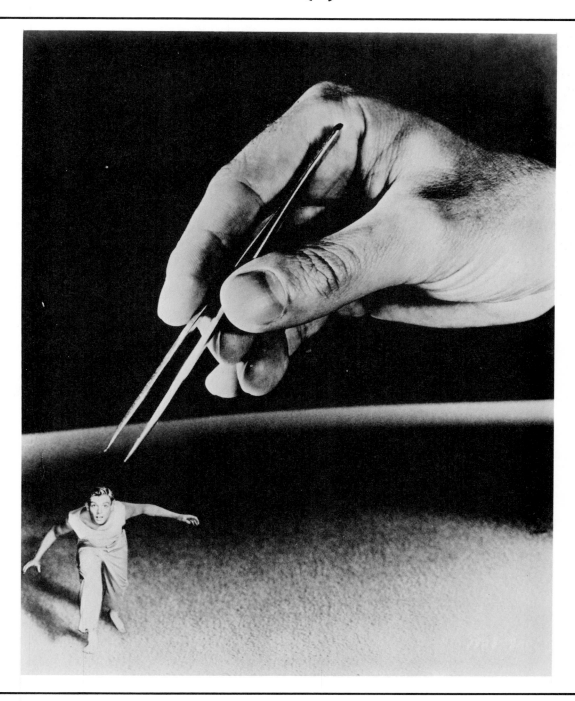

Attitudes to bullying

This is a graph drawn up by a class of 11 to 12-year-olds, consisting of an equal number of boys and girls, showing their attitudes to bullying. There were 28 children in the class at the time, and everyone voted 'yes' or 'no' to each question.

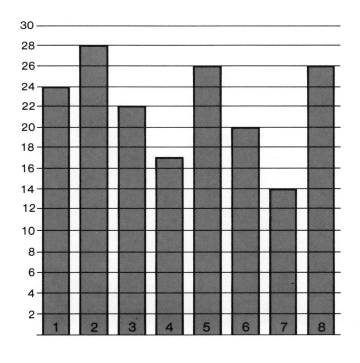

1. Have you ever been bullied?

2. Have you ever bullied others?

3. Do you think bullying is a serious problem in this school?

4. Should the school do more to stop bullying?

5. Have you seen much bullying at this school?

6. Do you think most bullying is only meant as a joke?

7. Do you think people often bully for money?

8. Do girls bully as much as boys?

Key
The vertical shows the number of pupils who answered 'yes', and the horizontal shows the number of the question.

Talking about the information on the graph

1 Do most people in the class think bullying is a serious problem?
2 How many pupils have *not* seen much bullying at school?
3 How many think the school should do more to stop bullies?
4 Which is the greater number — those who have been bullied, or those who have bullied others?
5 Do girls appear to be less likely to bully than boys?
6 According to this graph, does bullying seem to be a major problem in this particular school?

What causes bullying?

The class who prepared the graph on the previous page also discussed: what causes bullying? These are their suggestions. Discuss them together and choose the five best suggestions; put them in order of importance — the best one first. Then add a couple (or more) of your own suggestions. In the course of your discussion, look at the picture on p. 67. What does this seem to suggest about possible causes of bullying?

A   There are bullies because there are always some people who are bigger than others and love to push smaller people around.

B   There are bullies because there are always some people who are scared of other people.

C   There will always be bullies because it's human nature. You will never stop it.

D   You become a bully because you want to have your own back for something else (for example, if your parents upset you, you might go out and bully the little kid down the street).

E   People act like bullies when they think they can get away with it.

F   People are bullies because they like it. They think it's fun.

G   People are bullies because they want to show off. They think it makes them look good.

H   People bully each other when they are bored. It's because they have nothing else to do.

I   People become bullies because somebody else has bullied them.

J   Most bullies do not think they are bullies at all. They think they are doing the right thing. Lots of grown-ups (including teachers and parents) bully children, but they don't realise what they're doing.

On Aggression by Konrad Lorenz

After you have listened to and talked about the passage write your answers to these questions.

1 Does the writer think it is a good idea or a bad idea to keep a lot of cichlids in the same aquarium?

2 What happens if a pair of cichlids are left in an aquarium on their own?

3 The writer says that one method of saving the fish (when you have a pair on their own in an aquarium) is to put a scapegoat in with them. What does **scapegoat** mean?

4 The writer thinks there is a better way of saving the fish. What is it?

5 Does the writer think cichlids are naturally bullies or not?

6 What does the word **aggression** mean?

7 What does **spontaneous aggression** mean?

8 The passage is probably taken from
   a) a novel.
   b) a newspaper.
   c) a book about animals.
   Write down (a), (b) or (c).

9 The writer wants the reader
   a) to feel sorry for cichlids.
   b) to know how to look after cichlids.
   c) to think about how animals behave.
   Write down (a), (b) or (c).

10 The writer expects the reader
   a) to own an aquarium.
   b) to want to own an aquarium.
   c) to be interested in the way animals behave.
   Write down (a), (b) or (c).

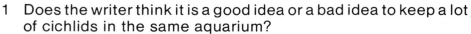

Punctuation: Full Stops and Capital Letters

Here are some extracts from reports written by pupils after listening to the passage by Konrad Lorenz. They are good reports, but check their punctuation and rewrite them without any mistakes. Do not alter the words.

1 the main point that konrad lorenz is making is that fish can , be bullies. Just like people can be For example cichlids will attack and even kill each Other.

2 The Only way to stop this is to keep pairs of cichlids together and to put other pairs. At the side of them. But you must have a glass partition between them

3 i was very interested in the book by konrad Lorenz it is all about the way animals fight

4 Cichlids are just like people if there are too many of them together they start Fighting. i think people are just like that

5 Konrad lorenz has studied the way animals start fighting he has compared this with the way people start fighting Also i can think of lots of people who are worse than animals they Fight for no reason at all.

A Case of Bullying

Two children are banned from the school premises in the lunch-hour, as a punishment for fighting. One of their parents writes to the school to complain. Are both pupils guilty? Are the facts what they appear to be? (Your teacher will tell you more about the situation.)

Suggestions for reading

Non-fiction:

Konrad LORENZ
King Solomon's Ring

A fascinating study of animals and of animal nature. Includes many examples of aggression and bullying among animals. See especially the chapters entitled *Robbery in the Aquarium, Poor Fish* and *Morals and Weapons.*

Konrad LORENZ
On Aggression

A study of animal behaviour, rather more difficult to read than *King Solomon's Ring* but just as rewarding. Note especially the chapters on *What Aggression Is Good For* and *The Spontaneity of Aggression.*

John SPARKS
Bird Behaviour

Well illustrated, short but informative. Looks at all aspects of bird behaviour including the bird's sense of territory and its ways of protecting the family. Good section on the bird's system of signalling anger, fear or intention to attack. Useful index and list of other books to read.

Fiction:

Bernard ASHLEY
A Kind of Wild Justice

The Bradshaw Brothers rule their part of the London underworld with a rod of iron. Four years ago they threatened to do Ronnie over if his father failed to toe the line, and Ronnie has lived ever since in terror of every ring at the doorbell. Now the Bradshaws are after another prize — the takings of the big football match on Saturday. Ronnie's Dad is needed to drive the getaway car and Ronnie, for the first time, is needed to help him.

John FOSTER (editor)
Gangs and Victims (collection of short stories)
Good set of stories about different aspects of gang life, with stories by Joan Tate, Shelagh Delaney and Evan Hunter, and others.

Alan GARNER
Elidor

Story of a world parallel to our own, that is threatened with destruction by evil forces — it can only be saved by four children who are able to move in and out of both worlds.

Suggestions for reading . . . continued

Brian GLANVILLE
A Bad Lot (and other stories)
Collection of stories about football and boxing — two of the toughest and most competitive sports. 'If they kick you, kick 'em back!' says one of the characters.

Thomas HUGHES
Tom Brown's Schooldays
Probably the most famous of all Victorian novels about school. Contains the notorious Flashman — perhaps the most loathsome bully in fiction!

Harold KEITH
Comanche!
The Comanches murdered his mother, took away his young brother, and made him their prisoner. Now Pedro lives as a Comanche. Only the strong survive and the weak are left to die. The warriors whip him like a dog but he grows hard and grows up — and then he falls in love with Willow Girl, who is married to another man.

Jack LONDON
The Call of the Wild
Story of a wolf-dog's life and nature, set in the wilds of Canada. Part of the same story as the same author's *White Fang,* and like the other novel, is concerned with the ways in which upbringing can influence character.

Margaret MAHY
The Haunting
Detective story with a difference. Barney is haunted by someone who is possibly still alive. His mother's family show no surprise and no one will explain what is happening. Then Tabitha and Troy set out to solve the mystery.

Sam McBRATNEY
A Dip of the Antlers
Barry Freeman takes school seriously, while 'Turk' Turkington is a regular truant. The two suddenly come to blows over a fountain pen. Neither boy wants to fight, but both feel they must. What begins as an ordinary playground fight soon develops into something serious.

7 TELLING STORIES (1)

Stories in Verse

There are many ways of telling a story. It can be written down — perhaps as a novel or short story — and it can be filmed. What other ways can you think of?

Reynard the Fox **is a long narrative poem about a fox-hunt.** *Narrative* **means telling a story.**

In this part of the poem the fox is finally hunted down after a long and exhausting chase.

Reynard the Fox

The fox was strong, he was full of running,
He could run for an hour and then be cunning,
But the cry behind him made him chill,
They were nearer now and they meant to kill.
They meant to run him until his blood
Clogged on his heart as his brush with mud,
Till his back bent up and his tongue hung flagging,
And his belly and brush were filthed with dragging.
Till he crouched stone-still, dead-beat and dirty,
With nothing but teeth against the thirty.
And all the way to that blinding end
He would meet with men and have none his friend:
Men to holloa and men to run him,
With stones to stagger and yells to stun him;
Men to head him, with whips to beat him,
Teeth to mangle, and mouths to eat him.
And all the way, that wild high crying.
To cold his blood with the thought of dying,
The horn and the cheer, and the drum-like thunder
Of the horsehooves stamping the meadows under.
He upped his brush and went with a will
For the Sarsen Stones on Wan Dyke Hill . . .

For a minute he ran and heard no sound,
Then a whimper came from a questing hound,
Then a 'This way, beauties', and then 'Leu, Leu',
The floating laugh of the horn that blew.
Then the cry again, and the crash and rattle
Of the shrubs burst back as they ran to battle,
Till the woods behind seemed risen from root,
Crying and crashing, to give pursuit,
Till the trees seemed hounds and the air seemed cry.
And the earth so far that he needs must die,
Die where he reeled in the woodland dim,
With a hound's white grips in the spine of him.
For one more burst he could spurt, and then
Wait for the teeth, and the wrench, and men.

John Masefield

For discussion

1 **Whose side does the poet want you to be on?**
2 **Whose side *are* you on?**
3 **What words or phrases make you feel**
   a) pity?
   b) anger?
4 **What happens at the end of this part of the poem?**

Stories in Drama

FRIENDS — extract from a television play by Colin Mack

Characters   Tommy
Mum

The scene is Tommy's home, early evening. Mum is getting supper ready for Dad. Tommy is doing some homework.

For a while nothing is said, then . . .

Mum   It's not right. I told you before.

Tom   But what have I done now?

Mum   You know what I'm talking about.

Tom   No.

Mum   The police! Why did the police come round here?

Tom   But we hadn't done anything. They said so themselves.

Mum   Afterwards. Yes, they said so afterwards. After they'd been round and frightened us to death. He's no good that boy, Mark what's-his-name. We told you before and we tell you again. For the last time. We do not want you to be friends with him.

Tom   Yeah.

Mum   What you doing now?

Tom   I'm doing my homework.

Mum   You pay attention. You can do your homework when I've finished talking to you.

Tom   Yeah.

Mum   Yeah what?

Tom   Yeah, Mum.

Mum   That's better. Well, do you promise me, then? Stop going around with that boy, that Mark? Your dad doesn't like it. I don't know what he'll do if I tell him you've been out with him again. Do you promise?

Tom   But he's all right. We don't do anything wrong.

Mum   Then why did the police suspect him for that business in the market? You tell me that! Well, I'll tell you. Because they knew about him already. In other words, he's got a record, that's what.

Tom   But it's not true. It's not fair. He hasn't got a record. He's no different from me or anyone.

Mum   He was on their list of suspects. And because you're his friend, his so-called friend, that put you on the list as well. And we have the

	police coming round to us. Well it's not right, and we're not having it. We've got your sister to think of as well as you. Don't you forget it.
Tom	Yeah.
Mum	Yeah! And what does that mean?
Tom	I don't know.
Mum	We've been too soft with you, that's our trouble.
Tom	He's all right — Mark — there's nothing wrong with him. We just go around together, that's all.
Mum	I don't like him. And that's final.
Tom	But the police made a mistake.
Mum	But how did he get on their books in the first place? That's what I want to know. In fact, I don't need to know. I can tell you. He's done something wrong before now, and that's how they know him. No surprise, is it. You've only got to look at him to know the sort of boy he is. Written all over him.
Tom	He's all right. He's my mate.
Mum	Then find another one. No more argument or I tell your father. And if he doesn't knock a bit of sense into you, I'll do it myself.
Tom	But, Mum —
Mum	No more 'buts'. That's the end of it.

For discussion

1 **What might happen next?**
2 **What might have happened before this scene began?**
3 **What sort of person is Mark?**
4 **What will be the attitude of Tom's dad?**
5 **What will Tom tell Mark — or will he tell him nothing about his mum's attitude?**

For improvisation

1 **Continue the scene, perhaps bringing dad into the play.**
2 **Improvise an earlier or later scene between the two friends.**
3 **Interview the characters.**

Stories in Prose

─────── { Jenny } ───────

The trouble started when Jenny developed the habit of staring. At first Paula paid no attention, she knew there was paint on her face and she did have a sty under her left eye. But her sty disappeared after a few days, and she'd made quite sure her face was clean. Jenny still went on staring at her. Every time she looked up from her book, she found Jenny staring straight at her as if she were a thing and not a person at all. Paula was beginning to feel unnerved by it, so she decided not to look at Jenny unless she had to.

She had forgotten all about it until she heard Gary going on about it last Friday afternoon in playtime. 'I'll do her if I catch her at it again. I'll do her.' He was glaring across the playground at Jenny who was picking cement out of the high brick wall by the road.

'What's she done?' Paula asked.

'Gawpin'. Staring — that's what. I've only got to look at her, just look that's all, and she's gawpin' back at me.'

'She can't be,' Rosemary said from behind him. 'She can't be all the time.'

'What d'you mean, she can't be?' Gary turned on her. 'I ought to know, oughtn't I? I ought to know when someone's staring at me. It's like Muhammad Ali before a fight. All morning she's been at it — like a zombie she is.'

'Well, it can't be all morning, not all morning,' Rosemary insisted. 'Because she was staring at me too, as if I had two heads or something. And that was all morning too — every time I looked up. So she couldn't have . . .'

'And me,' Paula interrupted. 'And me too. She was doing it to me as well you know.'

'I'll do her if she does it again,' Gary repeated. Gary was always 'doing' people — he wasn't much good at anything else, but no-one dared tell him so. After all he was the biggest boy in the school and a bully with a fearsome reputation, so everyone did what Gary said and steered well clear of him.

'I know,' said Rosemary, her voice dropping to a confidential whisper. 'I know — we'll stare her out. Like Muhammad Ali, like you said, Gary.'

'I'll do her,' Gary muttered. He wasn't listening.

'Let's stare her out first,' Paula said. 'And then you can "do" her afterwards — if it doesn't work, that is.'

The three friends try to stare out Jenny in class. But they end up falling asleep and getting into trouble. Later . . .

Paula picked up her anorak from the cloakroom and waited outside for Gary and Rosemary. Jenny walked past her, shrugging herself into her coat: there was a faraway look on her face, as if she were living in another world. It was that look that made Paula begin to wonder. Something strange had happened in the classroom: all three of them had tried to stare Jenny out, all three of them had fallen asleep. It could hardly be just a coincidence.

Rosemary came out. 'I tried,' Paula said. 'I really tried, but she wouldn't stop looking.'

'I don't understand it,' Rosemary said. 'She can't be looking at three places at once, can she? She can't be looking at you, me and Gary all at the same time, can she?'

'Perhaps Gary forgot,' Paula said. 'Perhaps it was just you and me.'

'He can't have. He was asleep, wasn't he? Just like us. She made us go to sleep, I know she did.'

'That's hypnotism,' Paula said.

'What's that mean?'

'It's when a doctor or a witch or someone like that sends you to sleep. They talk to you quietly and dangle a watch in front of your face.'

'But Jenny wasn't dangling . . .' Rosemary stopped short. There were angry shouts from the other end of the playground. They both knew who it was — there was only one boy who bellowed like that. They turned the corner to see a small crowd over by the brick wall.

Gary was standing head and shoulders above everyone else, and through the legs of the crowd they could see that there was someone lying on the ground. They barged through the crowd to get a better look. Gary was breathing heavily, his fists still held up to his chest and clenched hard. Jenny was lying on the ground with her coat torn off at the buttons, and there was blood running down her chin from her nose and falling on to her white blouse. No one was saying anything, they just gaped in stunned silence, and Jenny's face registered nothing, no pain, no anger, no fear, nothing. You could see Gary had been crying, and that seemed strange because there wasn't a scratch on him: he was standing there ready for more, and she was lying flat on her back against the wall with blood streaming from her nose.

Gary lowered his fists slowly, looked as if he was about to say something and thought better of it. He pushed his way past and began running. Jenny was getting to her feet, brushing the blood away from her chin so that it smeared upwards towards her eye. She was watching Gary as he ran out of

the school gates and disappeared across the road, and then she said in a quiet deliberate voice as expressionless as her face: 'I'll kill you.'

At Assembly on Monday morning there was a strange man on the plat-form next to Mr Penn. He didn't seem to know any of the hymns or prayers. He just stood there looking down over the rows of children and blowing his nose from time to time. He was one of those people who spring-clean their noses after every blow. Then Mr Penn kept making mistakes in the prayers. Everyone knew he was nervous in Assembly — you could see the prayer book shaking up and down in his hand, but he never made mistakes, not Mr Penn. Paula knew something was up and looked across to Rosemary who frowned back at her, tossing her head towards Gary's place by the radiator. Paula leaned forward. Gary's chair was empty, he wasn't there. She checked all around the hall, but he was nowhere. She felt Rosemary looking hard at her, and she didn't dare look back, she knew they were thinking the same thing. Jenny had done it, she must have done it. They looked over to Jenny's place. She was there, praying with her eyes tight shut.

Mr Penn was waving at them to sit down, and everyone was much quicker about settling down than usual.

'Good morning, children,' Mr Penn announced, straightening his tie as he always did. The chorus came back at him: 'Good morning, Mister Penn', it was more like a dirge than a greeting. 'Now, children, this is Chief Inspector Bridges from the Police Station. I want you all to listen very carefully to what he has to say. It's very important.' And Mr Penn stepped back carefully, sat down and crossed his legs.

The Police Inspector cleared his throat noisily and shuffled forward to the front of the platform. 'Can you hear me at the back?' he boomed out. No-one bothered to answer, no-one that is except for little Katie Doyle from the Infants who was sitting right under his feet. 'Yes,' she squeaked. Everyone laughed except Paula and Rosemary. They all hushed again.

'It's about Gary Hibben,' said the Inspector slowly. Paula felt her skin tingling all over her body. Jenny had done it, she really had gone and done it. 'Gary Hibben,' he repeated. 'Now you all know Gary, don't you?'

'Yes,' piped Katie again. No-one laughed this time.

'Well, Gary left school on Friday afternoon last, just like the rest of you, but he never went home — we don't know where he is.'

He paused and cleared his throat again. 'Now I've no doubt that we'll find him soon enough, but we can't do it without your help.'

Later . . .

Paula caught up with Rosemary by the drinking-fountain. 'I'm going to tell him,' she said. 'About the fight and what she said, and about her being a gypsy and everything. I'm going to tell him.' But Rosemary wasn't listening, she was gaping at the school gates and her mouth had dropped open as if she had seen a ghost. 'It's him,' she whispered. 'It's him.'

Gary was strolling in through the gate, a bag slung over his shoulder, and he was whistling ostentatiously. No-one else had seen him yet. They ran over to him and pulled him in behind the lavatory wall.

'Where've you been?' Rosemary was shaking him and there were tears pouring down her face.

'What happened?' Paula said. 'What did she do to you?'

'Happened? What did she do? What did who do? What you on about? Here let me go.' Gary pulled himself free.

'The police are here — they're looking for you.' Rosemary was calmer now.

'Police? The cops here? After me?' Gary sounded worried. 'What for? I done nothing wrong.'

'You never went home,' Rosemary said, pulling at him again. 'What happened?'

'Let go of me, will you.' He appeared to be thinking. 'Did dad tell them then?'

'He said you never went home,' Paula said.

'We thought . . .' Rosemary stopped herself.

'I've been up the football at Leeds, that's all. They can't get me for that, can they?'

'You should have told someone,' Paula said, forgetting who she was talking to.

'I couldn't, could I?' Gary said picking at his hand. 'Me dad said I mustn't go to football, not after all that trouble at Manchester. Said I wasn't old enough.' Gary was crying, you could hear it in his voice. 'I went anyway. I had to, everyone else was. And I can't go home, he'll do me, I know he will,' Gary sniffed, wiping his nose with the back of his hand.

Paula and Rosemary stayed in that afternoon to finish their writing on Leif the Lucky. Gary never bothered. He was too busy showing off in the playground; everyone wanted to bask in the reflected glory of big Gary Hibben who had been on the run from the police. And anyway, Fishiwick never even asked for the writing, she must have forgotten all about it.

They're still not sure about Jenny.

From *Jenny* **by Emma Langland**

For discussion

1 **Why does Jenny stare?**
2 **How does Jenny feel about Paula and her friends?**
3 **How will Gary handle his dad when he gets home?**
4 **How do the other children probably feel about Jenny? How do they feel about the three friends?**

For improvisation

1 **Interview some of the characters and try to find out all you can about their lives, families and attitudes.**
2 **Improvise some of the scenes from the story, or scenes that take place 'outside' the story, as for example when one of the children is at home.**

Vocabulary and Using a Dictionary

ANAGRAMS

An anagram is a word whose spelling is mixed up.
For example:

ROUDINSA is an anagram of DINOSAUR

Work out the following anagrams. They have all been
used in this unit or in earlier units.

1 **ROSHE**   2 **KOBO**   3 **PONSISYS**   4 **LUBLYING**

Choose some more words used in earlier units, and
turn them into anagrams. Try them out on the class or
on each other.

NONSENSE WORDS

One word in each of these groups is a nonsense word.
See if you can decide which one it is. Then use a dictionary to check that your answer is right.

1 GROGRAM	3 DODLE	5 PLUMBY
GUDGEON	DODDLE	PLUMBAGO
GUMBLE	DOODLE	PLUMULE
2 TAXIDERMIST	4 BEIGE	
TARDY	BILGE	
THUMPLE	BOMPER	

Invent some words of your own. Put them in a group of
words, and see whether the class can spot the nonsense words. Use a dictionary to help you.

All the following words have been used in earlier units. Without using a dictionary (until you have finished) choose the best answer for each one.

1 A legend is
  a) a popular story handed down from earlier times.
  b) a story that is made up.
  c) a story that everybody knows.

2 A synopsis is
  a) an instrument used by doctors.
  b) a story.
  c) an outline of a story.

3 A fossil is
  a) a kind of dinosaur.
  b) anything that is very old.
  c) the remains of something that existed long ago.

4 A carnivore is
  a) something used in carnivals.
  b) an animal.
  c) a flesh-eating animal.

5 A theory is
  a) a plan or idea.
  b) anything to do with religion.
  c) a lie.

6 A glossary is
  a) a kind of polish.
  b) a collection of animals.
  c) an alphabetical list of useful words.

Now check your answers in a dictionary.

Suggestions for writing

1 Play-writing

Write a part of the story *Jenny* as a play. Before you do this, look at the way in which the script of *Friends* is set out, on pp. 81–2.

If you wish, you can use some of the dialogue from the story itself.

Alternatively, write another scene for the play *Friends.*

2 Captions

When a picture is used in a book to illustrate a story, it usually has a *caption* underneath it. The caption is a short extract from the story. Look again at the illustrations on pp. 1, 15, 17, and 45, and invent captions to go with two of them.

3 Story-writing

Write a story to go with the illustration on p. 77 and use part of your story as a caption for the illustration.

Perhaps write the story as a poem.

Alternatively, write part of it as a poem and part of it in prose.

Suggestions for reading

Collections of short stories:

Authors' Choice (Books 1 and 2)
Anthologies of stories chosen by famous writers, including three contrasting stories of fantasy — Oscar Wilde's *The Happy Prince*, Ray Bradbury's *The Invisible Boy* and Arthur Porges' *The Ruum.*

Aidan CHAMBERS (editor)
The Devil's Bridge and other stories
Includes also *The World of Col Kelly* by Ray Jenkins, *The Invaders* by Henry Treece and *Sensor 249* by Christopher Leach.

Dennis PEPPER (editor)
Ends and Escapes
Includes *Seventeen Oranges* by Bill Naughton, *Marionettes Incorporated* by Ray Bradbury, and *Lamb to the Slaughter* by Roald Dahl.

Alan RIDOUT and James GIBSON (editors)
Supernatural
Includes *The Monkey's Paw* by W.W. Jacobs, *Bad Company* by Walter de la Mare, and *The Last Séance* by Agatha Christie.

P.J. ROBERTSON (editor)
Stirring Sea Stories
Includes *Problem at Sea* by Agatha Christie, *William and the Spy* by Richmal Crompton, and an extract from *The Poseidon Adventure* by Paul Galico.

Jean RUSSELL (editor)
Methuen Book of Sinister Stories
Twelve stories set in the present day and telling of strange and curious happenings. Includes *Mr Mushroom* (what *does* he keep locked up in the garden shed?) by Robert Swindells, and *Miss Hooting's Legacy* by Joan Aiken.

Novels:

Nina BAWDEN
Carrie's War
Albert, Carrie and Nick are wartime evacuees whose lives get so tangled up with the people they've come to live with, that the war and their real families seem to belong to another world — but then Carrie performs a fatal action that is to haunt her for years and years.

Leon GARFIELD
John Diamond
Young William Jones discovers that his dying father is a swindler. When he sets out for London to right the wrongs his father has done to his old partner, Diamond, he finds the back streets less welcoming and all kinds of horror lying in wait. Adventure story with an eighteenth century setting.

Suggestions for reading . . . continued

Michelle MAGORIAN
Goodnight Mr Tom

Willie is badly treated at home, but the Second World War breaks out and he is evacuated to the country. He stays with an old and unsociable widower who begins to care for him and teaches him how to enjoy life. But will his new-found happiness last? Or must he return to his own mother?

Philippa PEARCE
Tom's Midnight Garden

Tom was cross and resentful when his brother developed measles and he was sent away to stay with his aunt and uncle. He knew he would be bored and lonely. Then he made a strange and wonderful discovery — a discovery too fantastic for others to believe.

Sylvia SHERRY
A Pair of Jesus-Boots

Liverpool-bred Rocky dreams of becoming a real crook like his big brother, but when he actually gets involved with criminals it is only his sandals (his 'Jesus-boots') that save his life.

Catherine STORR
Marianne Dreams

When Marianne began to draw with a pencil that she found in an old work-box, she began to dream in a new way. She dreamed about what she drew. She drew a house, and that night she saw it in her dreams. She drew a boy in the window of the house and that night he was there too. Then her dreams started to get mixed up with the real world.

Narrative poems.
Here are some suggestions — all of them can be found in anthologies of poetry in your school library:

Anonymous, *Frankie and Johnny*
Robert Browning, *The Pied Piper of Hamlin*
T.S. Eliot, *Macavity, the Mystery Cat*
Wilfred Gibson, *Flannan Isle*
D.H. Lawrence, *Snake*
Walter de la Mare, *The Listeners*
John Masefield, *Reynard the Fox*
Alfred Noyes, *The Highwayman*
Robert Service, *The Shooting of Dan McGrew*
Alfred Tennyson, *The Lady of Shalott*

8 BULLYING (2)

HUNGRY

Black Boy *is the autobiography of Richard Wright. It is the story of his own childhood in the deep south of the USA in the early years of this century. His family were extremely poor, and they were even poorer when Richard's father left them.*

Hunger stole upon me so slowly that at first I was not aware of what hunger really meant. Hunger had always been more or less at my elbow when I played, but now I began to wake up at night to find hunger standing at my bedside, staring at me gauntly. The hunger I had known before this had been no grim hostile stranger; it had been a normal hunger that had made me beg constantly for bread, and when I ate a crust or two I was satisfied. But this new hunger baffled me, scared me, made me angry and insistent. Whenever I begged for food now my mother would pour me a cup of tea which would still the clamour in my stomach for a moment or two; but a little later I would feel hunger nudging my ribs, twisting my empty guts until they ached. I would grow dizzy and my vision would dim. I became less active in my play, and for the first time in my life I had to pause and think of what was happening to me.

'I'm hungry!' I said to my mother.
She was ironing and she paused and looked at me with tears in her eyes.
'Where's your father?' she asked me.
'I don't know,' I said.
'Who brings food into the house?'
'Papa,' I said. 'He always brought food.'
'Well your father isn't here now,' she said.
'Where is he?'
'I don't know,' she said.
'But I'm hungry,' I whimpered, stomping my feet.
'You'll have to wait until I get a job and buy food,' she said.

My mother finally went to work as a cook and left me and my brother alone in the flat each day with a loaf of bread and a pot of tea. When she returned in the evening she would be tired and dispirited and would cry a lot. Sometimes, when she was in despair, she would call us to her and talk to us for hours, telling us that we now had no father, that our lives would be different from those of other children, that we must learn to take care of ourselves, to dress ourselves, to prepare our own food; that we must take upon ourselves the responsibility of the flat while she worked. Half-frightened, we would promise solemnly. We did not understand what had happened between our father and our mother and the most that these long talks did was to

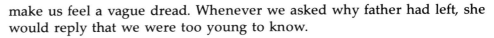

make us feel a vague dread. Whenever we asked why father had left, she would reply that we were too young to know.

One evening my mother told me that thereafter I would have to do the shopping for food. She took me to the corner store to show me the way. I was proud. I felt like a grown-up. The next afternoon I looped the basket over my arm and went down the pavement toward the store. When I reached the corner, a gang of boys grabbed me, knocked me down, snatched the basket, took the money, and sent me running home in panic. That evening I told my mother what had happened, but she made no comment; she sat down at once, wrote another note, gave me more money, and sent me out to the grocery again. I crept down the steps and saw the same gang of boys playing down the street. I ran back into the house.

'Don't you come in here,' my mother warned me.

From *Black Boy*

For discussion

1　About how old is Richard when these events take place? How can you tell?
2　Was this the first time he had been hungry?
3　Why does his mother send him out again with the money?
4　What do you think will happen next?

For writing

1　What different effects does hunger have upon Richard? Answer in words used in the passage.
2　Copy out a sentence or a part of a sentence from the passage to show that Richard's mother does not really know what to do to help her children.
3　Why did Richard's mother make no comment when she heard what had happened to the shopping-money?
4　This is an extract from an *autobiography* — explain what the word means.

Cloze Test

In the next part of the story, Richard is driven back by the gang several times and his mother tells him each time to defend himself. On this occasion she gives him a heavy stick and sends him out again, locking the door behind him.

Choose *one* word for each space.
Write out the numbers 1 to 10 underneath each other in your notebooks, and work together in pairs to decide which is the best word for each space.
Keep on re-reading the passage until you decide on your answers.

They surrounded me quickly and began to — (1) — for my hand. 'I'll kill you!' I threatened. They closed in. In blind — (2) — I let the stick fly, feeling it crack against a boy's skull. I swung again, lamming another skull, then another. Realising they would — (3) — if I let up for but a second, I fought to lay them low, to knock them —(4) —, to kill them so that they could not — (5) — back at me. I flayed with tears in my eyes, teeth clenched, stark fear making me throw every ounce of my — (6) — behind each blow. I hit again and — (7) —, dropping the money and the grocery list. The boys scattered, yelling, — (8) — at me in utter disbelief. They had never seen such — (9) —. I stood panting, taunting them to come and fight. When they refused, I ran after them, screaming. Their parents rushed into the streets, and for the first time in my life I shouted at grown-ups, telling them I would give them the same if they — (10) — me.

Read the passage again, and check that each word you have written down makes good sense.

Bullies in Schools

This is a report written by a pupil on the problem of bullying in schools.

He was asked to look especially at two questions. Firstly, what causes bullying? Secondly, how should bullies be punished?

In our school there are many bullies, and they never stop bullying. I think it is their nature to be bullies. They generally pick on children who are younger than they are, or who are polite and scared of them. They find real fun in bullying and they always thinks they are big and strong when they are doing it.

I think that bullies are really cruel and cowards. They are wrong to have a high opinion of themselves. They create vicious circles. They get together to cause nothing but trouble either by punching the younger children, or pinching their money, or pushing them on the ground, or making sarcastic remarks.

I think bullies should be reported to the teachers, and the school should keep records of them. They should be given one or two warnings and then a severe punishment. Their parents should be informed so that they have a clear picture of what is happening. If the parents cannot control their children, then the children should be expelled.

Every child should be encouraged to be brave and also to feel free to report bullies to the teachers. No child should be scared of them.

Amarjit, aged 11

For discussion

1 According to Amarjit, what causes bullying?
2 Do you agree with his opinions?
3 According to Amarjit, how should bullies be punished?
4 Do you think punishment would reduce the amount of bullying in schools?
5 What do you think Amarjit means when he says that bullies 'create vicious circles'?

For writing

There are four paragraphs in Amarjit's writing. Write down, in your own words, what you think is the main point made in each paragraph.

Here are two stories about bullying. They tell the same story from two different points of view. Only the beginning of the second story is given here. Read the stories and discuss:

a) how the writer shows the differences between the two story-tellers.

b) how the writer organises the first story in paragraphs, and how each paragraph shows a development in the story.

c) what will happen next in the second story.

The Day I Was Bullied

It was a cold, dark, dreary old morning when to school I went, walking very slowly. This morning I couldn't find anything to cheer me up. Then that thug Paul Roberts spotted me sulking in the corner of the playground out of the rain. He strode towards me confidently. I turned to run.

'Stay where you are, shrimp!' His words were cold and commanding. I stood rooted to the spot, knowing he wasn't going to let up on me. When he got to me, he stated 'You haven't paid the protection racket, have you?' I stood and said nothing. We were both getting soaking wet.

'Have you?' I still said nothing. Then, without another word, he struck me viciously across the face. I fell to the floor, reeling with pain. Then he started on me again. Suddenly a roll of lightning struck out, lighting the whole sky. Picking myself up, I breathlessly ran for the doors. His mob started to chase after me. The rain hindered them, but not much. When I got to the relative safety of the classroom, I slumped down on my stool and was just going to tell my teacher of my beating up, when I remembered that Paul would kill me if I told on him. So I just told the teacher I wanted to take the register. Then, walking to the office, I saw a notice saying, 'Tell us the names of the bullies and we'll help you!' I seriously believed this could work. If enough of us told on him, he might not try to bully us again. We had our lesson and then came playtime. I could not postpone it any longer. I went out at the pace of a snail. I went over to my friends and told them that if we all told on Paul, there'd be more evidence. A few of my friends volunteered but a lot were too scared to do a thing. We started across the wet playground that was almost waterlogged. It had stopped raining but it was still dark. Then he saw us. He stopped us dead in our tracks, but not for long. My friends and I sprinted away in terror and then his gang came in from all sides. We ran. Mark tripped over. We were going to stop for him but sheer terror made us run on. Mark got up, but was easily captured. Then we knew what procedure was coming. Holding Mark in a vice grip, Paul shouted, 'Ransom for Mark! Cheapest ever! 50p! If you don't pay, he gets tortured!'

While all this was happening Peter slipped away like a stealthy cat burglar. We emptied our pockets hurriedly. 40p was all we could manage. We knew Paul wouldn't hand him over for that, though we stared in sympathy and desperation for Mark. Then the torture began . . . Mark was starting to show signs of crying. Then along came good old Peter with a teacher. We all felt glee inside us. We were bursting with happiness that the bullies had been caught in the act. We explained to the teacher what had happened. He understood and took the boys away. We all felt fantastic. We all felt the sun was shining down on us, although it had just started raining again.

The Day I Was Caught

It was the kind of morning I loved when I walked through the school gates. The rain was tipping it down in buckets, the sky was dark, and I was going to bully someone. As the rain poured down the sky got darker and darker, and an angry cloud blotted out the light. I looked at myself in a window. My features were lit up in a strike of lightning. My black eye, which I had got the day before, looked funny on my face. My hair was shaggy as I hadn't brought a hood today. I walked briskly into the playground and met my friends. 'Any more protection money today?' I asked in a sharp voice . . .

Howard, aged 11

Three Poems

These three poems are in various ways on the theme of bullying.

A Case of Murder

They should not have left him there alone,
Alone that is except for the cat.
He was only nine, not old enough
To be left alone in a basement flat,
Alone, that is, except for the cat.
A dog would have been a different thing,
A big gruff dog with slashing jaws,
But a cat with round eyes mad as gold,
Plump as a cushion with tucked-in paws —
Better have left him with a fair-sized rat!
But what they did was leave him with a cat.
He hated that cat; he watched it sit,
A buzzing machine of soft black stuff,
He sat and watched and he hated it,
Snug in its fur, hot blood in a muff,
And its mad gold stare and the way it sat
Crooning dark warmth: he loathed all that.
So he took Daddy's stick and he hit the cat.
Then quick as a sudden crack in glass
It hissed, black flash, to a hiding place
In the dust and dark beneath the couch,
And he followed the grin on his new-made face,
A wide-eyed, frightened snarl of a grin,
And he took the stick and he thrust it in,

Hard and quick in the furry dark,
The black fur squealed and he felt his skin
Prickle with sparks of dry delight.
Then the cat again came into sight,
Shot for the door that wasn't quite shut,
But the boy, quick too, slammed fast the door:
The cat, half-through, was cracked like a nut
And the soft black thud was dumped on the floor.
Then the boy was suddenly terrified
And he bit his knuckles and cried and cried;
But he had to do something with the dead thing there.
His eyes squeezed beads of salty prayer
But the wound of fear gaped wide and raw;
He dared not touch the thing with his hands
So he fetched a spade and shovelled it
And dumped the load of heavy fur
In the spidery cupboard under the stair
Where it's been for years, and though it died
It's grown in that cupboard and its hot low purr
Grows slowly louder year by year:
There'll not be a corner for the boy to hide
When the cupboard swells and all sides split
And the huge black cat pads out of it.

Vernon Scannell

Beatings

My father beats me up
Just like his father did
And grandad he was beaten
by greatgrandad as a kid

From generation to generation
A poisoned apple passed along
Domestic daily cruelty
No one thinking it was wrong.

And it was:

Not the cursing and the bruising
The frustration and the fear
A normal child can cope with that
It grows easier by the year

But the ignorance, believing
That the child is somehow owned
Property paid for
Violence condoned.

by **Roger McGough**
from *Sky in the Pie*
published by Penguin (Kestrel Books),
1983

WILLY WET-LEG

I can't stand Willy wet-leg,
can't stand him at any price.
He's resigned, and when you hit him
he lets you hit him twice.

D. H. Lawrence

For discussion

1　**Why does the boy in** *A Case of Murder* **kill the cat?**
2　**How does he feel afterwards?**
3　**In Howard's story about the school-bully, he tells the story from two different points of view — the bullied boy's, and the bully's. Whose point of view is given in these poems?**
4　**Do the poems give any reasons why people bully?**

Report on Bullying

In this last section of the work on bullying you should review all the work you have done on the topic in this unit and also in Unit 6. The aim is to prepare a full written report on bullying, perhaps for presentation to another class for them to discuss or for presentation to the Headteacher. Your report could be divided into a number of sections:

1 **Our attitude to bullying**
This section should include the inquiries you made and the graph you drew up, when you were working on Unit 6, p. 69, together with your conclusions.

2 **Why do people bully each other?**
This section should include the work you did in Unit 6, p. 71, when you discussed this question, together with your conclusions.

3 **A case of bullying**
This section should include your report on the case of bullying from Unit 6, when you had to decide whether bullying had occurred and why.

4 **What can be done?**
Write briefly about anything you think the school might do to stop bullying, and explain why you think it might make an effect.

Suggestions for reading

The books recommended here continue to widen the theme of *bullying* to look at the place of aggression in human nature. In other words they ask the question, 'Are we all bullies of one kind or another?'

The first group of books deal with pre-historic times:

F. Clark HOWELL
The Search for Early Man

A large and comprehensive study, with a great range of information, ideal to browse through. See especially the chapter entitled *How the Savage Lives on in Man.*

Vincent MEGAW and Rhys JONES
The Dawn of Man

Detailed and informative. See especially the chapters on *Man Becomes Human, The Emergence of Modern Man* and *Modern Hunters.*

Eckehard MUNCK
Biology of the Future

Has an excellent chapter on *Stress* — look especially for the account of studies of a baboon named Boris, and of stress in rats. Deals also with the importance of sports and singing and dancing in getting rid of anger and aggression.

John NAPIER
The Origins of Man

Short and clear account of our evolution, with good illustrations and a helpful evolutionary tree showing our relationship to other species. Good sections on *Giants and Dwarfs, Man becomes a Hunter* and *Man Learns to Walk on Two Legs.*

C.H. and M. QUENNELL
Everyday Life in Prehistoric Times

Clear and detailed account of how people lived in prehistoric times. See especially the sections on the development of hunting skills. Good to browse through, and with a useful index.

Dorothy SHUTTLESWORTH
Real Book of Prehistoric Life

Good to browse through. See especially the chapters on *Famous Animal Ancestors, Real Man and a Reindeer,* and *Prehistoric Americans.*

Suggestions for reading . . . continued

The second group of books deal with later historical issues, and especially with medieval times.

Richard BARBER
Tournaments

Illustrated guide to the skills and weaponry of medieval tournaments. Includes sections on tournament rules, preparing for a tournament, armour for tournaments, and the last tournaments.

Ewart OAKESHOTT
Dark Age Warrior

Detailed account of a warrior's life in the age of legendary warriors such as King Arthur and Beowulf. Includes sections on swords and other weapons, styles of fighting, and an appendix on how to make replicas of helmets, swords and shields.

Mary C. BORER
Agincourt

Interesting account of a great battle, full of information about how people lived at the time and how they fought. See especially the chapters on *Preparations for War* and on *The Battle*. 'The ceremonial surrender was conducted with a terrible solemnity, designed to inflict the utmost humility on the defeated town . . . '

Grant UDEN
A Dictionary of Chivalry

Well illustrated, detailed reference book, with articles about every aspect of life in the so-called age of chivalry. A *Who's Who* and a *What's What!* See the articles especially on jousting and ransoms.

9 TELLING STORIES (2)

WHALE FISHING.

In the News

This unit gives some more examples of some of the different ways in which stories are told and written. The first four stories here are from *newspapers.*

Big hand for Big Claw

DINOSAUR hunter Bill Walker got a big hand from experts around the world yesterday.

A dinosaur skeleton that Bill, 55, found in a Surrey claypit was hailed as a discovery of 'enormous importance.'

Bill, a plumber from Thornton Heath, stumbled across a previously unknown species, now nicknamed Big Claw.

The dinosaur roamed the marshes of Southern England about 125 million years ago.

It was up to 15ft tall, weighed about two tons and could run as fast as 20 mph.

The first part of the creature that Bill spotted was one of its huge claws, believed to have been used to kill its prey.

The rest of the remains were excavated by a team headed by Dr Allen Charig, of the Natural History Museum, in London.

Dr Charig said: 'The find has excited us considerably. This is the first record of any meat-eating dinosaur being found in rock of this age anywhere in the world'.

GIANT: How the dinosaur may have looked

BUS FARE FOR WHITE MOUSE

Local schoolgirl Linda Farrell was today charged an extra fare of sevenpence for the white mouse she was carrying in a small white box.

The incident occurred when Linda, travelling with her grandfather, was asked by the conductor to explain the squeaks coming from the box. When she told him it was her four-week-old pet mouse, the conductor checked the regulations and told her the mouse counted as livestock and livestock must be paid for.

Linda refused to pay the extra money, but after some delay, when the driver refused to take the bus any further until the fare was settled, Linda's grandfather paid the money for her. Linda's parents say, 'We are disgusted with the whole thing, and intend to complain to the Bus Company.'

Marmaduke Goes Home

Marmaduke Gingerbits was back home last night nine months after a fight began to prove who owned him.

The Bow County Court in East London decided that Marmaduke really is Marmaduke, a ginger tom-cat, and that he belongs to Mr and Mrs J. Sewell.

Mr Monty Cohen thought he was really another cat called Sonny, and that he belonged to him. But the judge said he was wrong.

Marmaduke left the court with a blanket covering his cage. He had been the star witness during the trial and was often taken into the witness box.

The case cost £6000 and the lawyers now have to work out who pays what.

MOUSE'S BUS FARE REFUNDED

NEB Bus Company officials, at their monthly meeting, today agreed to refund to Linda Farrell (and her grandfather) the sevenpence bus fare demanded for her white mouse.

An official spokesman said the conductor had acted properly and conscientiously in charging the fare, but that the Company did not classify a white mouse as livestock. 'It is too small', said the spokesman.

The Company have written to Linda offering her the refund any time she calls in to the Company offices. But Linda's grandfather says that the money should be sent through the post. 'It will cost us more than that in bus fares to go down and collect the refund', he said.

Questions on the news stories

1 Who was the chief witness in the case of Marmaduke Ginger-bits?
2 According to Mr Cohen, what is Marmaduke's real name?
3 According to the judge, what is Marmaduke's real name?
4 Find *one word* in the story about Marmaduke that means 'a person who has seen something happen'.
5 For what reason was Linda asked to pay the fare for the white mouse?
6 Who actually paid the fare?
7 According to the Bus Company, should the conductor have asked Linda to pay a fare for the mouse?
8 Has the bus fare been paid back?
9 What exactly did Bill Walker see?
10 How old is the dinosaur's skeleton?
11 What does *excavated* mean?
12 Find *one word* in the story about the dinosaur that means 'a group of related animals'.
13 Some newspapers are national newspapers — they are read all over the country. Some are *local* newspapers — they are read only in the town where they are written. Which of these stories are taken from a local newspaper? Which are taken from a national newspaper? How do you know?
14 Complete the following sentence with *one* word only:
    'All four stories have one thing in common: they are all about — .'

Novels

Probably the most popular way of reading stories is through reading novels.

A *novel* is a long story, written down.

So far, what is the best novel you have read?

What is the most popular novel in the whole class?

Novels are works of *fiction;* this means that they do not claim to be true. But many novels are *based on* fact — can you think of any examples?

Check the meanings of both words — *novel* and *fiction* — in a dictionary.

Little House in the Big Woods

a novel by Laura Ingalls Wilder

Laura lives on the prairies of America with her mother and father and her two sisters, Mary and Carrie. Their farm is a long way from the nearest town.

Laura was proud to be helping Ma with the milking, and she carried the lantern very carefully. Its sides were of tin, with places cut in them for the candle-light to shine through.

When Laura walked behind Ma on the path to the barn, the little bits of candle-light from the lantern leaped all around her on the snow. The night was not yet quite dark. The woods were dark but there was a grey light on the snowy path, and in the sky there were a few faint stars. The stars did not look as warm and bright as the little lights that came from the lantern.

The next part of the story is written here with the sentences in the wrong order. Work out the right order.

A   She lived in the barn.

B   It was too early in the spring for Sukey to be let out in the Big Woods.

C   Ma was surprised too.

D   Now Ma and Laura saw her behind the bars, waiting for them.

E   Laura was surprised to see the dark shape of Sukey, the brown cow, standing at the barnyard gate.

F   But sometimes on warm days, Pa left open the door of her stall, so she could come into the barnyard.

The next part of the story is written here with the paragraphs in the wrong order. Work out the right order.

A Just then one of the dancing bits of light from the lantern jumped between the bars of the gate, and Laura saw long, black fur, and two little glittering eyes. Sukey had thin, short, brown fur. Sukey had large gentle eyes.

B Ma said, 'Laura, walk back to the house.'
So Laura turned around and began to walk towards the house. Ma came behind her. When they had gone part way, Ma snatched her up, lantern and all, and ran. Ma ran with her into the house and slammed the door.

C Ma went up to the gate and pushed against it to open it. But it did not open very far, because there was Sukey standing against it. Ma said, 'Sukey, get over!' She reached across the gate and slapped Sukey's shoulder.

The story continues with the paragraphs still in the wrong order. Work out the right order.

D Ma finished mending the shirt. Laura saw her fold it slowly and pause. She smoothed it with her hand. Then she did a thing she had never done before. She went to the door and pulled the leather latch-string through its hole in the door, so that nobody could get in from outside unless she lifted the latch.

E Then she put supper on the table for Laura and Mary. Pa had not come home yet. He didn't come. Laura and Mary undressed, and they said their prayers and snuggled into bed.

F She saw that Laura and Mary were still awake, and she said to them, 'Go to sleep, girls. Everything is all right. Pa will be back here in the morning.'

G Then Laura said, 'Ma, was it a bear?'
'Yes, Laura,' Ma said, 'it was a bear.' Ma was trembling, and she began to laugh a little. 'To think,' she said, 'I've slapped a bear!'

H Ma sat by the lamp, mending one of Pa's shirts. The house seemed cold and empty and strange without Pa.

When you have agreed on the right order, re-read the whole extract together.

The Breadwinner

The parents of a boy of fourteen were waiting for him to come home with his first week's wages.

The mother had laid the table and was cutting some slices of bread and butter for tea. She was a little woman with a pinched face and a spare body, dressed in a blue blouse and skirt, the front of the skirt covered with a starched white apron. She looked tired and frequently sighed heavily.

The father, sprawling inelegantly in an old armchair by the fireside, legs outstretched, was little too. He had watery blue eyes and a heavy brown moustache, which he sucked occasionally.

These people were plainly poor, for the room, though clean, was meanly furnished, and the thick pieces of bread and butter were the only food on the table.

As she prepared the meal, the woman from time to time looked contemptuously at her husband. He ignored her, raising his eyebrows, humming, or tapping his teeth now and then with his finger-nails, making a pretence of being profoundly bored.

'You'll keep your hands off the money,' said the woman, obviously repeating something that she had already said several times before. 'I know what'll happen to it if you get hold of it. He'll give it to me. It'll pay the rent and buy us a bit of food, and not go into the till at the nearest public-house.'

'You shut your mouth,' said the man, quietly.

'I'll not shut my mouth!' cried the woman, in a quick burst of anger. 'Why should I shut my mouth? You've been boss here for long enough. I put up with it when you were bringing money into the house, but I'll not put up with it now. You're nobody here. Understand? *Nobody. I'm* boss and he'll hand the money to me!'

'We'll see about that,' said the man, leisurely poking the fire. Nothing more was said for about five minutes.

Then the boy came in. He did not look older than ten or eleven years. He looked absurd in long trousers. The whites of his eyes against his black face gave him a startled expression.

The father got to his feet.

'Where's the money?' he demanded.

The boy looked from one to the other. He was afraid of his father. He licked his pale lips.

'Come on now,' said the man. 'Where's the money?'

'Don't give it to him,' said the woman. 'Don't give it to him, Billy. Give it to me.'

The father advanced on the boy, his teeth showing in a snarl under his big moustache.

'Where's that money?' he almost whispered.

The boy looked him straight in the eyes.

'I lost it,' he said.

'You — *what?*' cried his father.

'I lost it,' the boy repeated.

The man began to shout and wave his hands about.

'Lost it! *Lost* it! What are you talking about? How could you lose it?'

'It was in a packet,' said the boy, 'a little envelope. I lost it.'

'Where did you lose it?'

'I don't know. I must have dropped it in the street.'

'Did you go back and look for it?'

The boy nodded. 'I couldn't find it,' he said.

The man made a noise in his throat, half grunt, half moan — the sort of noise that an animal would make.

'So you lost it, did you?' he said. He stepped back a couple of paces and took off his belt — a wide, thick belt with a heavy brass buckle. 'Come here,' he said.

The boy, biting his lower lip so as to keep back the tears, advanced, and the man raised his arm. The woman, motionless until that moment, leapt forward and seized it. Her husband, finding strength in his blind rage, pushed her aside easily. He brought the belt down on the boy's back. He beat him unmercifully about the body and legs. The boy sank to the floor, but did not cry out.

When the man had spent himself, he put on the belt and pulled the boy to his feet.

'Now you'll get off to bed,' he said.

'The lad wants some food,' said the woman.

'He'll go to bed. Go and wash yourself.'

Without a word the boy went into the scullery and washed his hands and face. When he had done this he went straight upstairs.

The man sat down at the table, ate some bread and butter and drank two cups of tea. The woman ate nothing. She sat opposite him, never taking her eyes from his face, looking with hatred at him. Just as before, he took no notice of her, ignored her, behaved as if she were not there at all.

When he had finished the meal he went out.

Immediately he had shut the door the woman jumped to her feet and ran upstairs to the boy's room.

He was sobbing bitterly, his face buried in the pillow. She sat on the edge of the bed and put her arms about him, pressed him close to her breast, ran her fingers through his disordered hair, whispered endearments, consoling him. He let her do this, finding comfort in her caresses, relief in his own tears.

After a while his weeping ceased. He raised his head and smiled at her, his wet eyes bright. Then he put his hand under the pillow and withdrew a small dirty envelope.

'Here's the money,' he whispered.

She took the envelope and opened it and pulled out a long strip of paper with some figures on it — a ten shilling note and a sixpence.

Leslie Halward

For discussion

1 **Which characters do you have sympathy with?**
2 **Which characters does the writer have sympathy with?**
3 **How did you expect the story to end?**
4 **Is there anything about the father that makes you feel at all sorry for him?**
5 **Is this as good a story as *Jenny* (pp. 83–7)?**

Punctuation — Speech Marks

There are parts of most stories where people speak to each other.

These are shown by *speech marks.*

For example: She said, "It's time to go home."

Notice the use of *commas:*

> A comma is used before the words that are spoken, for example when we write:
>> He said, "I'm scared."
>
> A comma can also be used after the words spoken, for example when we write:
>> "I'm scared," he said.

Notice too the use of *capital letters:*

> What is said always begins with a capital letter, even though it may not be the beginning of a sentence.

For example:

> Jack said, "That's a clever thing to say."

Re-read *The Breadwinner* **and look especially at the way the writer uses speech marks to show who is speaking and what is said.**

Rewrite the following with speech marks.

1 Mr Smith said, I should hardly think that he'll come tonight.
2 Mum called out, Charlie, I've told you to come home.
3 He cried out, I'm scared. I'm scared.
4 He won't come tonight, Mr Smith said.
5 I've told you to come home, Charlie, Mum called out.

Re-write the following with speech marks and commas:

1 God frowned, and the tortoise said I want a skin.
2 I cannot give you what you ask for said God.
3 The tortoise replied Then make one please!
4 God asked him Do you want a beautiful skin?
5 I don't mind if it is beautiful or ugly said the tortoise.

Rewrite the following with speech marks, commas and capital letters:

1 Charlie came in and said it's been a long day.
2 We've been very worried about you said his mother.
3 But there was no need to worry said Charlie.
4 His mother was very angry and told him you must never come home late like this again.
5 You should have been home hours ago said his father.

As an exercise in punctuation, make up a very short conversation between two people — perhaps between two friends on their way to school — and check that you use speech marks, capital letters and commas correctly.

Notice that you should start a new line every time the speaker changes, and should also start about 25 millimetres in from the margin as if you were beginning a new paragraph. Notice how this is done in *The Bread-winner.*

For example:
  "Come on now," said the man.
  "Don't give it to him," said the woman. "Don't give it to him, Billy. Give it to me."

NB   When you write speech marks it is better to use double marks (i.e. "Yes." *). However, you will often find that books use single speech marks (i.e.* 'Yes.'). *In fact you will usually find them printed that way in this book.*

A Case of Blackmail

A parent has written to the school to complain that a pupil has been blackmailed (or forced in some way) to pay money to another pupil. Both pupils give different stories, and two other pupils give different stories again. Who is telling the truth? What has happened? (Your teacher will tell you more about the situation.)

Suggestions for writing

Look at the illustrations on pp. 93 and 107 and use one of them as the basis of one or more of the following:

A newspaper story.
A poem.
A short story.
A play.
A part of a novel.

Write a caption to go with the illustration you have chosen.

Suggestions for reading

Collections of short stories:

Roger Lancelyn GREEN (editor)
Ten Tales of Adventure

Includes stories about Catherine de Medici, the French Revolution and the Napoleonic Wars. Authors include John Buchan, Rudyard Kipling, R.L. Stevenson and Stanley Weyman.

Alan JENKINS (editor)
Mystery

Anthology of 21 baffling stories, including stories about mysterious wigs, a priceless vase, and Adolf Hitler. Authors include W.B. Yeats, Conan Doyle, G.K. Chesterton and H.G. Wells.

Alan JENKINS (editor)
This Sporting Life

Anthology of stories about many different sports, including sky-diving, falconry, jousting and mountain-climbing. Authors include Ernest Hemingway, H.G. Wells and P.G. Wodehouse.

Flora Annie STEELE
Tales from the Punjab

Excellent collection of Indian folk tales and legends. Includes *The Wrestlers, The Jackal and the Crocodile, The Son of Seven Mothers* and *Prince Lionheart and his Three Friends.*

The Times Anthology of Children's Stories

Collection of stories submitted in 1973 for *The Times Children's Story* competition. Includes *The Luggage,* by Alison Fenton; *Ben and the Winter Warmer* by Edgar Jones; and *But You Promised* by Josephine Lee — a story that begins: 'This morning I bit Miss Chandler. She was surprised. So was I . . . '

A. WILLIAMS-ELLIS and M. OWEN (editors)
Out of this World

Collection of science fiction stories. Authors include Isaac Asimov (*Living Space*), Arthur C. Clarke (*Who's There?*) and Brian Aldiss (*Hothouse*).

Novels:

Gillian AVERY
Call of the Valley

Sam Williams goes back to his farm in the Welsh hills and his uncle throws him out and accuses him of theft. Sam is now all on his own, with no one to turn to.

Suggestions for reading . . . continued

Enid BAGNOLD
National Velvet

A girl with a passion for horses wins a horse in a raffle. She trains it and then races it in the Grand National.

Paul BERNA
A Hundred Million Francs

The adventures of a gang of Parisian children. They set out to find the villain who has stolen their tricycle and meet the clever M. Sinet, Inspector of Police.

Roy BROWN
Undercover Boy

When Chips Regan, a policeman's son, goes in search of his lost Labrador pup down the river, he gets caught up in the activities of a gang of runaway kids who are helping a jewel thief to flee the country.

John CHRISTOPHER
Empty World

Neil Miller goes to live with his grandparents when all his family are killed in a car crash. Then a deadly virus sweeps the world, leaving Neil more alone than ever. Can he cope entirely on his own?

Penelope LIVELY
The Revenge of Samuel Stokes

Tim Thornton and his family move into a new housing estate and learn it was built on the site of Chanstock Park, a garden designed in the eighteenth century by Samuel Stokes. Mysterious things start happening, and Tim and his friend Jane decide to find out why.

10 WORDS

One Word . . . Many Meanings (1)

Words mean different things to different people. As a simple example, the dentist's chair means quite different things to

a patient in the waiting room;

a dentist seeing to a patient;

a cleaner at work in the surgery;

a craftsman who makes the chair;

a removal man who has to pick it up.

Talk together about the different people for whom the following would have quite different meanings:

Piano

Fish

Medicine.

Here is an example of the different ways in which different people write about *fog!*

POETS write about fog.

The fog comes
On little cat feet;
It sits looking over harbour and quay
On silent haunches;
And then moves on.

Carl Sandburg

The yellow fog that rubs its back upon the window-panes,
The yellow smoke that rubs its muzzle on the window-panes,
Licked its tongue into the corners of the evening,
Lingered upon the pools that stand in drains,
Let fall upon its back the soot that falls from chimneys,
Slipped by the terrace, made a sudden leap,
And seeing that it was a soft October night,
Curled once about the house, and fell asleep.

T. S. Eliot

A PUPIL writes about fog in a geography lesson.

Fog is not as common as rain or snow. It is dangerous. It can cause accidents. It can make people ill. It can make us lose our way. There are places where there is a special kind of fog called smog. This is like fog but it is caused by the fumes from motor cars. The city of Los Angeles in the United States of America has terrible smog, and it is there all the time. It never goes away.

A METEOROLOGIST writes about fog.
(Check the word **meteorologist** in a dictionary.)

Fog is simply a cloud that forms near the earth. Ground fogs often form at night in damp places, after the earth has used up the heat of the day. Fogs may also form when warm, damp air blows over the cool earth at night, or over the cool sea. The fog consists of very small drops of water, millions and millions of them, swirling through the air. If these little drops hit a surface they stick to it, whether it is a window-sill, a coat collar, or a person's hair.

Adapted from *The Weather* **by Time-Life Books**

A STORY-TELLER writes about fog.

I am not easily scared. Strange noises at night, being alone in an empty house, the sudden knock of a stranger on my door — all these things do nothing to me. I remain cool and sensible and calm. So I was deeply surprised to find myself so frightened when, returning home from school one winter evening, a very heavy fog surrounded me and I lost my way. There were times when I could hardly see my hand in front of my face. Indeed I spent some time amusing myself by testing how far I could move my hand without losing sight of it. But then, in playing this simple game, I suddenly touched something I could not see, something damp and warm and large . . .

From *Night Stories* **by Robin Hammond**

For discussion

1 **What different effects do these writings have on their readers?**
2 **What does the first poem compare fog to?**
3 **What does the second poem compare it to?**
4 **What word is often used by the story-teller but is not used by the meteorologist or by the geography pupil?**

The Poet's Words

Poets are often able to make a great impression on the reader or listener while using few words. In poetry (and in other writing too, at times) a little can say a lot. At times this is because the poem brings vivid pictures to the reader's mind.

Here are three poems and a prayer, all to some extent on the same theme.

JABBERWOCKY

'Twas brillig, and the slithy toves
   Did gyre and gimble in the wabe;
All mimsy were the borogoves,
   And the mome raths outgrabe.

'Beware the Jabberwock, my son!
   The jaws that bite, the claws that catch!
Beware the Jubjub bird, and shun
   The frumious Bandersnatch!'

He took his vorpal sword in hand:
   Long time the manxome foe he sought —
So rested he by the Tumtum tree,
   And stood awhile in thought.

In *Jabberwocky* the poet mixes sense and nonsense. Make a list of the words that the poet has invented. Which ones are the most effective or amusing?

This is the remainder of the poem. Working in pairs, invent words of your own to fill in the spaces. Before you do this, talk about the number of *syllables* in each line and make sure that you invent words that have the right number of syllables to keep the rhythm of each line.

> **NB 'Syllable' means part of a word.**
> **PAPER has two syllables, 'pa' and 'per'.**
> **TELEVISION has four syllables, 'te', 'le', 'vi' and 'sion'.**

And as in uffish thought he stood,
  The Jabberwock, with eyes of flame,
Came whiffling through the — (1) — wood,
  And burbled as it came!

One, two! One, two! And through and through
  The vorpal blade went snicker-snack!
He left it dead, and with its head
  He went — (2) — back.

'And hast thou slain the Jabberwock?
  Come to my arms, my — (3) — boy!
O — (4) — day! Callooh! Callay!'
  He chortled in his joy.

'Twas brillig, and the slithy toves
  Did gyre and gimble in the wabe;
All mimsy were the borogoves,
  And the mome raths outgrabe.

Lewis Carrol

For discussion

1 **Make a list of the words invented by the class.**
2 **Which are the most suitable for the poem?**
3 **How do they compare with the words used by the poet himself?**

THINGS IN THE DARK

I am fearful, not of the dark
But of darkness,
Harbouring things unknown, unseen.
Now I can laugh and make merry
In the shafts of welcome sunlight
Filtering through tender green leaves.
But a storm cloud obliterates the warmth and light:
The world becomes unnaturally dark;
The silhouetted trees sway vigorously
In the gathering gloom.

Now is the time for fear:
Fear of entering the depths of the forest,
Of being mauled and molested
By foul things, unnamed.
The adrenalin flows.
I run blind through the black trees . . .
All is light once more.
I have reached the border of the forest.
Fear is gone —
Until darkness comes again.

Amanda, aged 13

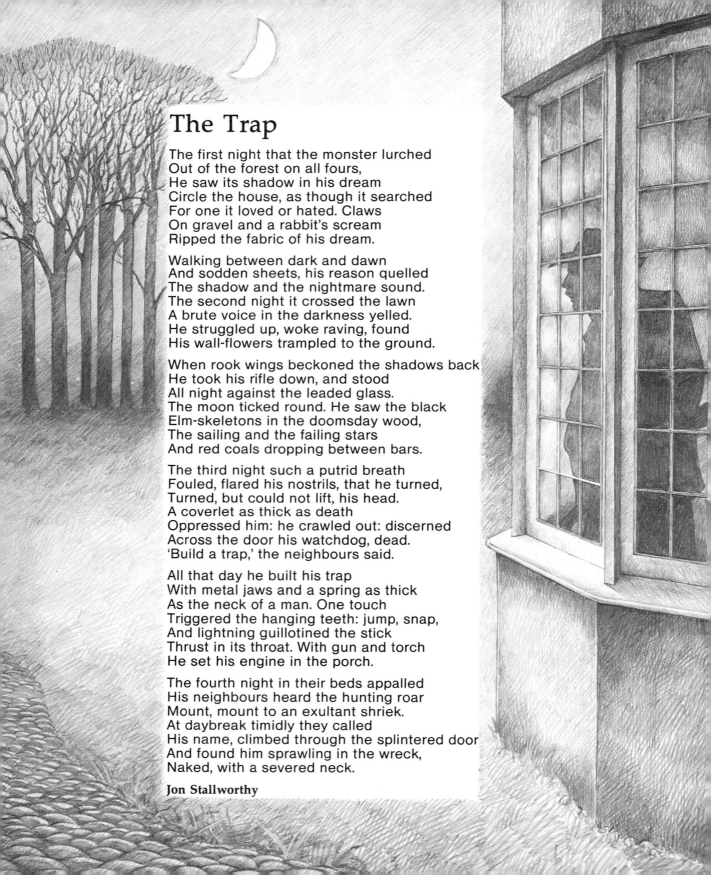

The Trap

The first night that the monster lurched
Out of the forest on all fours,
He saw its shadow in his dream
Circle the house, as though it searched
For one it loved or hated. Claws
On gravel and a rabbit's scream
Ripped the fabric of his dream.

Walking between dark and dawn
And sodden sheets, his reason quelled
The shadow and the nightmare sound.
The second night it crossed the lawn
A brute voice in the darkness yelled.
He struggled up, woke raving, found
His wall-flowers trampled to the ground.

When rook wings beckoned the shadows back
He took his rifle down, and stood
All night against the leaded glass.
The moon ticked round. He saw the black
Elm-skeletons in the doomsday wood,
The sailing and the failing stars
And red coals dropping between bars.

The third night such a putrid breath
Fouled, flared his nostrils, that he turned,
Turned, but could not lift, his head.
A coverlet as thick as death
Oppressed him: he crawled out: discerned
Across the door his watchdog, dead.
'Build a trap,' the neighbours said.

All that day he built his trap
With metal jaws and a spring as thick
As the neck of a man. One touch
Triggered the hanging teeth: jump, snap,
And lightning guillotined the stick
Thrust in its throat. With gun and torch
He set his engine in the porch.

The fourth night in their beds appalled
His neighbours heard the hunting roar
Mount, mount to an exultant shriek.
At daybreak timidly they called
His name, climbed through the splintered door
And found him sprawling in the wreck,
Naked, with a severed neck.

Jon Stallworthy

OLD CORNISH PRAYER

From ghoulies and ghosties
And long-leggety beasties
And things that go bump in the night
Good Lord deliver us!

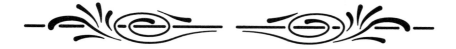

For discussion

1 Check the words used in *The Trap.* Are there any difficult or unusual words? (For example, 'lurched'.) Talk about what the difficult words probably mean, and then check them in a dictionary.

2 In *The Trap,* what happens on each of the four nights?

3 What could the unknown monster have been?

4 Choose a couple of words or phrases from each poem that you find interesting or imaginative.

Word-Games

Many poems play with words, have fun with the language. *Jabberwocky* **is an example.**
Try some of these word-games.

1 Alliteration

An *alliteration* is a short (or long) list of words beginning with the same sound:

> pretty Polly Perkins, or
> shivering shattered Shirley.

Take the first names of everyone in the class, and working on your own or in pairs, write a *Who's Who* of the class using as many alliterations as you can think of to describe each person.

2 Nonsense-nouns

Nouns are one of the main 'parts of speech' which we put together to make a sentence. Often nouns represent a person, a place or a thing. For example,

> The girl ran into the playground.

Both *girl* and *playground* are nouns.
An example of a nonsense-noun would be, for example,

> The girl saw the *bomble* in the playground.

Complete each of these sentences with a nonsense-noun of your own.

> Kate asked me if she could borrow my — (1) —. She said she did not have hers with her. She thought she had left it in the — (2) —. I told her I would never lend anyone my — (1) —, not even my best friend. But I would lend her my — (3) —. This made her angry and she said that I had a spare — (1) — in my — (4) —. I told her she was wrong about this, and that what I had in my — (4) — was a — (5) —.

3 Anagrams

An *anagram* is a word whose spelling has been muddled up, so that all the letters are in the wrong order. There were examples of these in Unit 7.

All these anagrams are taken from words in the poems in this Unit.

What are the actual words?

ratcere (From the poem by T. S. Eliot.)
oghutht (From *Jabberwocky.*)
nedskars (From Amanda's poem.)
nights (From the prayer.)
rasts (From *The Trap,* verse 3.)

Choose words from the writings about 'fog' and turn them into anagrams of your own.

Test them on each other.

The Origins of Words

The English language has been very much influenced by other languages. For example, many English words are derived from Latin (the written language of ancient Rome). Here are a few examples.

AQUA   **was the Latin word for** *water.*
          English words derived from aqua include *aquarium and aquatic.*

TERRA   **was the Latin word for** *earth.* **English words derived from it include** *territory* **and** *terrain.*

Here are some more Latin words. See if you can think of a couple of English words derived from each one. They do not have to keep the exact meaning of the Latin.
Use a dictionary to help you.

Thinks . . . video

FEMINA	=	woman
CIRCA	=	round about
VIDEO	=	see
AUDIO	=	hear
VICTUS	=	conquered
SCHOLA	=	leisure, rest from work
SATIS	=	enough
LIBER	=	free
HOSTIS	=	enemy
MAGNUS	=	large

The Changing Language

New words are brought into the language. Old words fade out. Words change from time to time — in their meaning, in their sound, in their spelling. For example, here is an extract from Geoffrey Chaucer's *Canterbury Tales*. These are a collection of two dozen stories told to each other by a group of pilgrims as they ride together from London to Canterbury. Chaucer wrote them in the late fourteenth century.

This extract comes from *The Prologue*, where the writer introduces each of the pilgrims. At this point he has just described a knight, and now he describes the knight's son — a young squire.

Although this was written 600 years ago, most of it is not too difficult for a modern reader to make sense of it.

With him ther was his sone, a young SQUIER,
A lovyere and a lusty bacheler,
With lokkes crulle as they were leyd in presse.
Of twenty yeer of age he was, I gesse.
Of his stature he was of evene lengthe,
And wonderly delivere, and of greet strengthe.
And he hadde been somtime in chivachie
In Flaundres, in Artois, and Picardie,
And born him weel, as of so litel space,
In hope to stonden in his lady grace.
Embrouded was he, as it were a meede
Al ful of fresshe floures, white and reede.
Singinge he was, or floytinge, al the day;
He was as fressh as is the month of May.
Short was his gowne, with sleves longe and wide.
Wel koude he sitte on hors and faire ride.
He koude songes make and wel endite,
Juste and eek daunce, and weel purtreye and write.
So hoote he lovede that by nightertale
He sleep namoore than dooth a nightingale.
Curteis he was, lowely, and servisable,
And carf biforn his fader at the table.

For discussion

1 How many words can you find in this extract that we still use but which we spell differently?
2 Can you find any words that we no longer use?

One Word . . . Many Meanings (2)

Many words can mean different things at different times. Everything depends on how and where they are used. For example, in these sentences the word *catch* means two different things.

a) He tried to catch the ball.

b) He could not solve the problem — there was a catch to it.

What are the two meanings of *catch* that are used here? Here are some more examples from words used in this unit.

1 A word in the pupil's essay on fog can mean
   a) often seen, or
   b) low or cheap.
   What is the word? What does it mean here?

2 A word is used in the meteorologist's extract to mean not warm or almost cold.
   It is also used in the storyteller's writing about fog to mean relaxed, or not worried.
   What is the word?

3 A word in *Jabberwocky* can mean
   a) a part of the mouth, or
   b) chats or gossips.
   What is the word? What does it mean here?

4 A word in the pupil's essay on fog can mean
   a) similar to, or
   b) almost love.
   What is the word? How is it used here?

5 A word in the same essay can mean
   a) sort or type, or
   b) pleasant or good-natured.
   What is the word? What does it mean here?

Suggestions for writing

1 Invent the name of an animal, person or object. Invent more words to describe it (for example, what it does or where it lives or what it looks like). Put these together to make up some kind of story — perhaps do this as a poem.

2 Write a short prayer for use, for example, when coming to school, or before a particular lesson, or when going to the dentist.

3 Make a list of some of the things that frighten you and choose two or three ways of describing how you feel about them; put the list together as a poem.

4 Make a list of words and phrases that capture the mood and feeling of the illustration on p. 123. Then choose the three or four that you think are the best.
Do the same with the illustration on p. 137.

5 Choose a topic such as
   a) anger.
   b) bullying.
   c) sunshine.
   d) sharks.
Write briefly about the one you chose in a number of different ways such as
   a) a poem.
   b) a newspaper story.
   c) a short story.
   d) an article for an encyclopaedia.

Suggestions for reading

These books explore language from a number of starting-points, including the 'language' of animals and the connections between different languages.

Colin BLAKEMORE
A Burning Fire

Collection of essays on different aspects of language, including an account of the attempts of two American psychologists to teach chimpanzees how to talk. A difficult book, but worth browsing through.

Gerald DURRELL
The Drunken Forest

Collection of accounts of life with a variety of creatures in the South American jungles. See especially the chapter on Sarah Huggersack — 'One of the nicest things about the jays was their incessant chattering . . . They would spend hours on their perches facing each other and with raised eyebrows carrying on the most involved conversations . . . They were great mimics and in a few days had added the barking of dogs to their repertoire.'

Eric HAWKINS
Spoken and Written Language

Good introductory report on early kinds of writing, the development of the alphabet and the importance of spelling. Good final section on how to test your STM (short-term memory).

J.D. CARTHY
Animal Behaviour

Large, informative and well illustrated. Interesting account of teaching rats to distinguish between different kinds of sign and of chimpanzees learning to use tools to reach food outside their cages. There is also a good discussion about whether animals can add up!

Gerald DURRELL
Encounters with Animals

Includes accounts of animals as inventors, as architects and as fighters. Worth looking especially at the story of the fight between a wild black rat and a bombadier beetle.

Clive JENKINS
Language Links — The European Family of Languages

Good introductory account of the ways in which the English language is linked to other languages, including the links with Latin, Greek and Indian Sanskrit.

Barry JONES
How Language Works

Asks, 'Why do we need language?' Shows how we discover patterns in our language and how these patterns work for us. Useful final section on how to go about learning a foreign language.

Suggestions for reading . . . continued

National Geographic Magazine (October 1978)

Excellent article and pictures about Koko the gorilla.

Mike RALEIGH
The Languages Book

Very good introduction to the questions, 'What is language? How does it 'work'? How does it develop?' Published by the English Centre of the Inner London Education Authority.

John SPARKS
The Discovery of Animal Behaviour

Detailed, informative and well illustrated. Ideal for browsing. Sections on *Animal Learning* and on *Signs and Signals*. Worth looking especially for an account of how the worker-bee tells her companions where to find nectar-rich flowers by performing a waggle-dance.

J.W. TIBBLE and Anne TIBBLE
Helen Keller

True story of Helen Keller who went blind and deaf when she was 2 years old. No one could teach her anything until her family engaged Joanna Sullivan as her governess.

TIME-LIFE BOOKS
The Birth of Writing

Large, well illustrated, ideal for browsing. With sections on the first alphabet, the earliest kinds of writing and the education of Babylonian scribes — 'Long before the stiff examination that ended the ordeal of school, many a student had dropped out . . . The best that such an outcast could expect for all his trouble was a humble post as a village letter writer.'

11 SCHOOL RULES

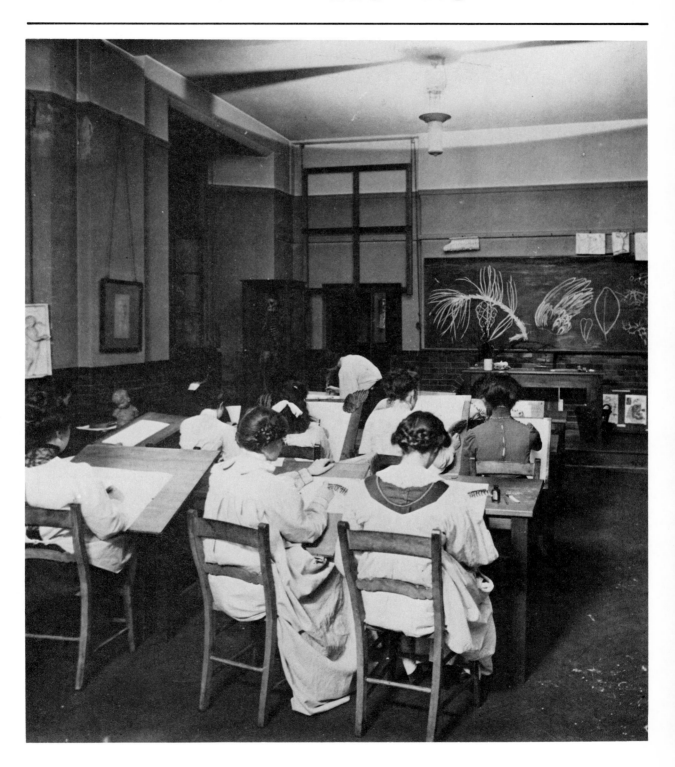

Rules for Pupils in the USSR

In Russia every child is expected to *know* **and to** *obey* **all the following rules.**

1 To acquire knowledge persistently in order to become an educated and cultured citizen and to be of the greatest possible service to my country.
2 To study diligently, to be punctual in attendance, and not arrive late for classes.
3 To obey the instructions of the school director and the teachers without question.
4 To arrive at school with all the necessary textbooks and writing materials; to have everything ready for the lesson before the teacher arrives.
5 To come to school clean, well-groomed, and neatly dressed.
6 To keep my place in the classroom neat and tidy.
7 To enter the classroom and take my place immediately after the bell rings; to enter and leave the classroom during the lesson only with the teacher's permission.
8 To sit upright during the lesson, not leaning on the elbows or slouching; to listen attentively to the teacher's explanation and other pupils' answers, and not to talk or let my attention wander to other things.
9 To rise when the teacher or director enters or leaves the room.
10 To stand to attention when answering the teacher; to sit down only with the teacher's permission; to raise my hand if I wish to answer or ask a question.

Before you read the remaining rules, discuss the following:
1 **Are any of your own school rules included here?**
2 **Which, if any, of the Russian rules should be included in your own school rules?**

11 To take accurate notes in my assignment book of homework scheduled for the next lesson, and to show these notes to my parents, and to do all the homework unaided.

12 To be respectful to the school director and teachers; when meeting them to greet them with a polite bow; boys should also raise their caps.

13 To be polite to my elders, to behave modestly and respectfully in school, in the street, and in public places.

14 Not to use coarse expressions, not to smoke, not to gamble for money or other objects.

15 To protect school property; to be careful of my personal things and the belongings of my comrades.

16 To be attentive and considerate of old people, small children, the weak and the sick; to give them a seat on the bus or make way for them in the street, being helpful to them in every way.

17 To obey my parents, to help them take care of my small brothers and sisters.

18 To maintain order and cleanliness in rooms; to keep my clothes, shoes and bed neat and tidy.

19 To carry my student's record book with me always, to guard it carefully, never handing it over to anyone else, and to present it on request to the teacher or school director.

20 To cherish the honour of my school and class and defend it as my own.

For discussion

1 Are there any rules on the Russian list which you think would *not* work in your own school?

2 Are there any rules in your own school which do not work because so few people obey them?

3 Choose the five most important rules from the Russian list, and the five most important rules in your own school. Arrange them in order of importance with the most important one first. (Take *important* to mean that the rule helps pupils to work well and enjoy their work at school.)

4 Are there any rules in your school which most people obey even though they are not written down and nobody ever told you about them?

5 Do schools need rules?

Vova Neglects his Maths

In the USSR, groups of pupils are elected by the rest of the pupils to keep an eye on everyone's progress. They meet every week and talk about any pupil who is not working well.

Here is an account of one such meeting — it is adapted from *Two Worlds of Childhood* by Urie Bronfenbrenner, published by Allen and Unwin in 1971.

The passage is reproduced here with some words left out. Read it through and choose *one* word for each space.

It was Friday afternoon and the class council were — (1) — to discuss each pupil in the class. They gave a — (2) — from one to five for all aspects of a pupil's work, including such things as cleanliness and sports. The final mark was — (3) — on a slip of paper to be given to the pupil, who then had to take it home and ask a parent to — (4) — for it.

The young members of the — (5) — took their job seriously. They were talking about Sasha, editor of the class newspaper. Lyolya, who was in charge of the council, asked for their — (6) — . One of the pupils thought that recent — (7) — of the newspaper had not been very good. 'Then, let's give him a 4 instead of a 5,' said one of the pupils. 'That may make him try harder.'

The next — (8) — was more difficult. A month ago, Vova had been — (9) — that he was doing badly in arithmetic and pulling down the class. There had been no improvement.

After some discussion, Lyolya said, 'I think this is serious enough to require action by the entire class. We can call a special meeting for this afternoon.'

At the class meeting, Vova, a handsome lad in a white shirt, was — (10) — forward, and asked what he did yesterday when he got home from school.

The rest of the passage is given here with the last ten sentences in the wrong order.
Write out the numbers 1 to 10 underneath each other in your notebooks, and work out the right order for the sentences.

'As always, I cleaned house so that Mother would not have to do it when she got home. Then I did my homework.'

'What subjects?'

'English, history, some drawings.'

As no mention was made of maths, the class looked at each other.

A   'I suggest that we choose two of our class to look after Vova while he does his maths homework,' said a girl with a blue hair ribbon.

B   Then Lyolya looked sternly at Vova.

C   Vova replied, 'I did not have any maths homework last night.'

D   Vova said, 'I don't need them, for I promise I can do it by myself.'

E   'You should have studied some maths anyway,' said another voice from the class.

F   'A month ago we told you to work harder at maths, and now you do not even mention it,' said Lyolya.

G   Lyolya asked the class for recommendations.

H   Lyolya was not impressed.

I   'Now two of your classmates will work with you, and when they say you are ready to work alone, we'll believe it.'

J   'We have seen what you do by yourself,' said Lyolya.

YOUTH IN SPARTA

Listening Comprehension

148

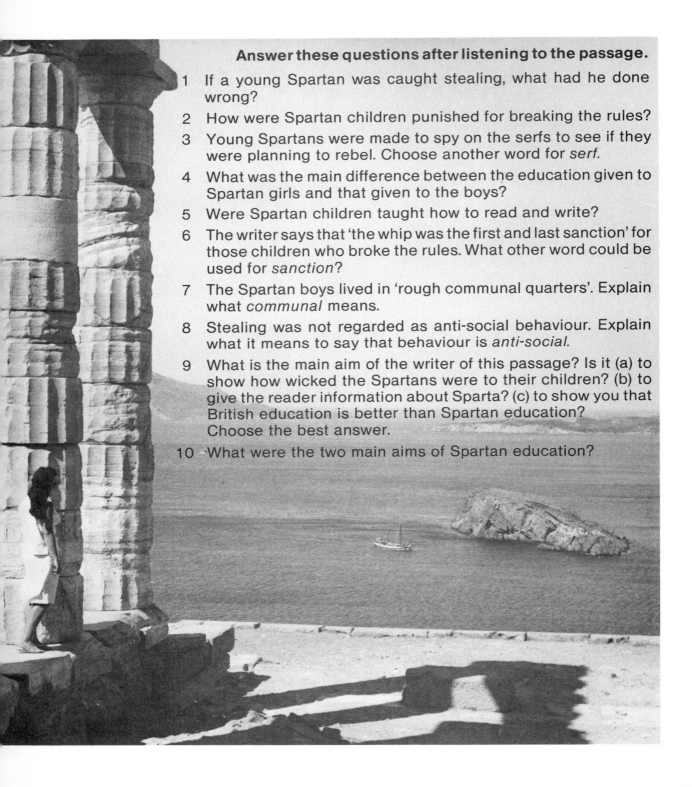

Answer these questions after listening to the passage.

1 If a young Spartan was caught stealing, what had he done wrong?

2 How were Spartan children punished for breaking the rules?

3 Young Spartans were made to spy on the serfs to see if they were planning to rebel. Choose another word for *serf*.

4 What was the main difference between the education given to Spartan girls and that given to the boys?

5 Were Spartan children taught how to read and write?

6 The writer says that 'the whip was the first and last sanction' for those children who broke the rules. What other word could be used for *sanction*?

7 The Spartan boys lived in 'rough communal quarters'. Explain what *communal* means.

8 Stealing was not regarded as anti-social behaviour. Explain what it means to say that behaviour is *anti-social*.

9 What is the main aim of the writer of this passage? Is it (a) to show how wicked the Spartans were to their children? (b) to give the reader information about Sparta? (c) to show you that British education is better than Spartan education? Choose the best answer.

10 What were the two main aims of Spartan education?

Questionnaire on Schooling

What are your views on these questions? Discuss them, and choose the answer that is closest to your own opinion.

1 At what age should children start school?

   a 3 to 4. ☐

   b 5 to 6. ☐

   c 7 to 8. ☐

2 If you had to make a choice, would you send your child to

   a a selective school where you have to pass an entrance exam? ☐

   b a comprehensive school? ☐

   c a boarding school? ☐

   d no school at all? ☐

3 How much should parents have to pay for their child's schooling?

   a Nothing (apart from what they already pay in taxes). ☐

   b A little. ☐

   c What they can afford. ☐

   d The entire cost. ☐

4 Should decisions about children's education be made by

   a the government? ☐

   b the schoolteachers? ☐

   c the parents? ☐

   d the pupils? ☐

   e a combination of all these? ☐

5 If a child is not successful at school is this mainly the fault of

   a the parents? ☐

   b the teachers? ☐

   c the child? ☐

   d all of these? ☐

   e none of these? ☐

6	Which of these should be compulsory lessons for all children?	**a** Sports.	☐
		b Religion.	☐
		c Mathematics.	☐
		d Any subject not mentioned here.	☐
7	What is the most important thing a child learns at school?	**a** Reading, writing and arithmetic.	☐
		b Learning to get along with others.	☐
		c Learning to think for himself/herself.	☐
		d Something else.	☐
8	When a teacher is, in your opinion, a good teacher is it because	**a** he/she knows his/her subject well?	☐
		b the pupils like him/her?	☐
		c the teacher understands his/her pupils?	☐
		d of something else?	☐
9	When a child does something wrong, should the teacher	**a** hit the child?	☐
		b give the child 'lines'?	☐
		c keep the child in detention after school?	☐
		d talk severely to the child?	☐
		e do something else?	☐
10	When a child keeps on doing something wrong, should the teacher	**a** hit the child?	☐
		b send the child to the Head?	☐
		c write to the parents?	☐
		d discuss the matter with other teachers?	☐
		e do something else?	☐

1 Compare your answers around the class, making a note of the number of people choosing each answer.

2 What are the most *controversial* questions — that is to say, which are the ones about which you most disagree?

3 Note the three most controversial questions, and working in small groups, discuss them. Explain your own opinion, and encourage the others to tell you theirs. See if any of your opinions change.

4 Write a report on your discussions, choosing the three or four questions that most interest you. Explain which answer most people chose, and which answer you chose, and explain why you chose it.

One way of setting out your report would be:

Sentences, Full Stops and Capital Letters

Here are some extracts from pupils' writing on the questionnaire. They are reproduced here as they were written.

1 What corrections would you make to them?
2 What is good about the way they are written?
3 Rewrite them with any corrections you think necessary.

Question 1   At what age should children start school?

We talked a lot about this question most people thought it is a good thing to start at 5. This is when most of us started school. However Desmond said that in very cold countries they often start school at 8 or 9 this is because children in the very cold countries often live a long way from their schools. So if they have a long way to go, it is better to let them get older before they have to go to school. I pointed out that in a country like England there are some children who live a long way from school. I asked desmond if he thought those children should start school later than the rest of us . . .

Question 6   What lessons should be compulsory for all children?

Sunita said that Maths and English should be compulsory and most of us agreed with her. George, on the other hand, thought Physical Education was more important than anything else I was not sure about this I am not much good in P.E., and I cannot see what good it does me desmond however said it would do me a lot of good if i tried harder. it is important because it keeps you fit . . .

Question 8   What should the teacher do when the child does something wrong?

Most people think the teacher should talk severely to the child sunita said this is the fair thing to do. It makes the child feel sorry so she will behave better next time but a lot of people disagreed with this. For example. Desmond said that talking severely to most children does no good a lot of children just laugh when a teacher talks severely to them the teacher must do something worse than that . . .

Word-Games

In Unit 10 there were some word-games, with alliterations, nonsense-nouns and anagrams. Check and revise, what is
a) alliteration?
b) a noun?
c) an anagram?
Here are some more.

1 Synonyms and antonyms

A *synonym* is a word meaning the same as another word. For example, *pleasant* can be a synonym for *nice*. An *antonym* is a word meaning the opposite of another. For example, *ugly* can be an antonym of *beautiful*.

mirror, mirror on the wall...

See how many synonyms and how many antonyms you can find for these words.

    tough
    sometimes
    great
    frightful
    excitement

2 **Nonsense-verbs**

A *verb* is any word that is used in a sentence to show something that *is done* or something that *is*.
For example,

The boy is a good dancer. The girl dances well too.
Both *is* and *dances* are verbs.
An example of a *nonsense-verb* would be

The boy *bombles* better than the girl does.
Complete each of these sentences with a nonsense-verb of your own.

The teacher was angry when he saw the boy — (1) — . When he told him off for it, the boy said he was only — (2) — . 'There's no harm in — (2) — ,' said the boy. However, the teacher said he had definitely seen the boy — (1) — and so he reported him to the Head. When the Head heard about this she — (3) — . She was so annoyed she sent for the Deputy Head and — (4) — him. They decided to call a special meeting of all the teachers in the school and — (5) — about it.

3 **Similes**

A simile is a comparison between two very different things. Ordinary speech is full of similes. For example,

He was *as white as a sheet.* George dances *like an elephant.*

Invent some similes of your own. You can include a few non-sense ones. Perhaps make a list of things and complete them with similes. For example,
She was a marvellous dancer, as light as . . .
Amarjit came into the room like . . .
The rain came down like . . .

4 **Nonsense-nouns and nonsense-verbs**

Re-read the short passage from (2) above, beginning *The teacher was angry when he saw . . .* Make a list of all the *nouns* in the passage. Compare your list with the rest of the class. Then choose four of the nouns and invent nonsense-nouns to replace them. Finally, rewrite the passage with nonsense-verbs and nonsense-nouns.

Suggestions for reading

Many novels have been written about school-life. These are just a few suggestions that you might enjoy dipping into:

F. ANSTEY
Vice Versa

Mr Bultitude expresses the wish that he could be young again and go back to school. As he says this, he happens to be holding the magical Garuda Stone and his wish is immediately granted. His son Dick, who does not like school at all, seizes the stone and wishes to be changed into his father. Mr Bultitude is sent off to school, and Dick is left at home to do what he likes.

Gerald DURRELL
My Family and Other Animals

Not a novel, strictly speaking, but a memoir of an entertaining family who went to live on a Mediterranean island and of the remarkable things that young Gerald learned about without going to school.

Gene KEMP
Charlie Lewis Plays for Time

Adventures of the Moffett family and their encounter with a new teacher who believes in silence, discipline and the inferiority of girls — 'No girl is good enough to play cricket!'

Phil REDMOND
Grange Hill Stories

A collection of stories about various characters. Includes The Mystery of the Missing Gnomes and A Question of Uniform — 'What should you do when you see Dracula, Frankenstein's Monster, four werewolves, two vampires and the Incredible Hulk all in one room? Keep your fingers crossed and hope that it's a fancy dress party.'

P.G. WODEHOUSE
Mike, and Enter Psmith

'Are you the Bully, the Pride of the School, or the Boy who takes to drink and is led astray in Chapter Sixteen?' Psmith asks Mike on arriving at Sedleigh School. And, 'If you ever have occasion to write to me, would you mind sticking a P at the beginning of my name? P - s - m - i - t - h. See?'

There are many books about schools and education at different times in history. Here are some suggestions for browsing through:

Kenneth ALLEN
One Day in Tutankhamun's Egypt

Portrays the lives of a range of different characters in Egypt in 1350 B.C. They include a soldier, a stone mason, a priest and a schoolboy.

Suggestions for reading . . . continued

E.R. CHAMBERLIN
Everyday Life in Renaissance Times

Looks at the lives of the rich and the poor, scholars, knights, labourers, artists and apprentices. Well illustrated and with a section on education: 'Richard II . . . decreed that any parent in his kingdom was free to send his child to school — if a school could be found.'

Alfred DUGGAN
Growing Up in the 13th Century

Explores the lives of different classes of people — peasants, craftsmen, merchants, earls. Has a good section on education: 'Boys would continually drop out of grammar school . . . If they were stupid or even slow, they would not be able to bear the incessant beating.'

E.W. HEATON
Everyday Life in Old Testament Times

Detailed and well illustrated. Includes sections on military life and also on education: 'The average boy of Isaiah's time never went to school; in fact the Old Testament has no word for school . . . '

Joan LIVERSIDGE
Everyday Life in the Roman Empire

Very good section on education, and especially on the grammar school, where, 'Poetry, mythology, history, geography . . . were carefully studied so that a store of general knowledge was acquired.'

R.I. PAGE
Life in Anglo-Saxon England

Detailed, and with good illustrations. Interesting sections on *A Woman's Place* and *The Working Man*. Briefly portrays the harsh life of a child in a monastery school: 'The questioner asks if the lad has had a beating that day . . . and he replies, "No, because I was wary!" '

M. and C. QUENNELL
Everyday Things in Ancient Greece

Good to browse through, detailed, and with black and white illustrations. Section on *Life Inside the House* and with various references to education: girls were mostly kept 'under the strictest restraint, so that they might see as little, hear as little, and ask as few questions as possible.'

12 AUTOBIOGRAPHICAL

Points of View

Every story is told from a point of view. In some stories the point of view changes while the stories are being told.

What are the different points of view from which these stories (or extracts from stories) are told?

The Secret Brother

Jack lived in the green-house
When I was six,
With glass and with tomato plants,
Not with slates and bricks.

I didn't have a brother,
Jack became mine.
Nobody could see him,
He never gave a sign.

Just beyond the rockery,
By the apple-tree,
Jack and his old mother lived,
Only for me.

With a tin telephone
Held beneath the sheet,
I would talk to Jack each night.
We would never meet.

Once my sister caught me,
Said, 'He isn't there.
Down among the flower-pots
Cramm the gardener

Is the only person.'
I said nothing, but
Let her go on talking.
Yet I moved Jack out.

He and his old mother
Did a midnight flit.
No one knew his number:
I had altered it.

Only I could see
The sagging washing-line
And my brother making
Our own secret sign.

Elizabeth Jennings

AN EXTRACT FROM BLACK BEAUTY

I was now beginning to grow handsome; my coat had grown fine and soft and was bright black. I had one white foot, and a pretty white star on my forehead. I was thought very handsome; my master would not sell me till I was four years old; he said lads ought not to work like men, and colts ought not to work like horses till they were quite grown up.

When I was four years old, Squire Gordon came to look at me. He examined my eyes, my mouth, and my legs; he felt them all down; and then I had to walk and trot and gallop before him. He seemed to like me, and said, 'When he has been well broken in he will do very well.' My master said he would break me in himself, as he should not like me to be frightened or hurt, and he lost no time about it, for the next day he began.

From *Black Beauty* **by A. Sewell**

For discussion

1 **Does the point of view of the story-teller make a difference to the story? Would** *The Secret Brother* **have been different if the story-teller had been** *Jane* **or** *she* **instead of** *I***? Would the second story have been different if it had been** *he* **instead of** *I***?**

2 **Re-read the two stories from a different point of view — for example a friend's (in the poem) or the Squire's (in the second story). Is there a difference?**

Cowboy Song

I come from Salem County
  Where the silver melons grow,
Where the wheat is sweet as an angel's feet
  And the zithering zephyrs blow.
I walk the blue bone-orchard
  In the apple-blossom snow,
When the teasy bees take their honeyed ease
  And the marmalade moon hangs low.

My Maw sleeps prone on the prairie
  In a boulder eiderdown,
Where the pickled stars in their little jam-jars
  Hang in a hoop to town.
I haven't seen Paw since a Sunday
  In eighteen seventy-three
When he packed his snap in a bitty mess-trap
  And said he'd be home by tea.

Fled is my fancy sister
  All weeping like the willow.
And dead is the brother I loved like no other
  Who once did share my pillow.
I fly the florid water
  Where run the seven geese round,
O the townsfolk talk to see me walk
  Six inches off the ground.

Across the map of midnight
  I trawl the turning sky,
In my green glass the salt fleets pass,
  The moon her fire-float by.
The girls go gay in the valley
  When the boys come down from the farm,
Don't run, my joy, from a poor cowboy,
  I won't do you no harm.

The bread of my twentieth birthday
  I buttered with the sun,
Though I sharpen my eyes with lovers' lies
  I'll never see twenty-one.
Light is my shirt with lilies,
  And lined with lead my hood,
On my face as I pass is a plate of brass,
  And my suit is made of wood.   **Charles Causley**

The Streets of Laredo

As I walked out in the streets of Laredo,
As I walked out in Laredo one day,
I spied a young cowboy all wrapped in white linen,
All wrapped in white linen as cold as the clay.

'I see by your outfit that you are a cowboy' —
These words he did say as I boldly stepped by,
'Come sit down beside me and hear my sad story;
I'm shot in the breast and I know I must die.

'It was once in the saddle I used to go dashing,
Once in the saddle I used to go gay;
First to the ale-house and then to the jail-house,
Got shot in the breast and I'm dying today.

'Get six jolly cowboys to carry my coffin;
Get six pretty maidens to carry my pall;
Put bunches of roses all over my coffin,
Roses to deaden the clods as they fall.

'Oh, beat the drum slowly and play the fife lowly,
Play the dead march as you carry me along;
Take me to the green valley and lay the sod o'er me,
For I'm a young cowboy and I know I've done wrong.

'Go gather around you a crowd of young cowboys
And tell them the story of this, my sad fate;
Tell one and the other before they go further
To stop their wild roving before it's too late.

'Go fetch me a cup, a cup of cold water
To cool my parched lips,' the cowboy then said.
Before I returned, the spirit had left him
And gone to its Maker — the cowboy was dead.

We beat the drum slowly and played the fife lowly,
And bitterly wept as we carried him along;
For we all loved our comrade, so brave, young and handsome,
We all loved our comrade although he'd done wrong.

Anonymous

For discussion

1 **From what point of view is** *Cowboy Song* **told?**
2 **What different points of view are shown in the set of stories in this unit so far?**
3 **Working in groups, re-read all three poems to each other.**
4 **Which poem do you like best?**

About Ourselves

**The three extracts in this section are autobiographical.
And they are all set in America in the 20th century.**

I KNOW WHY THE CAGED BIRD SINGS

*This is a black woman's account of growing up in the South of the USA, in the 1920s.
She lived mostly with her grandmother, who owned the local store, and with her
brother, Bailey, who was a year older than herself.*

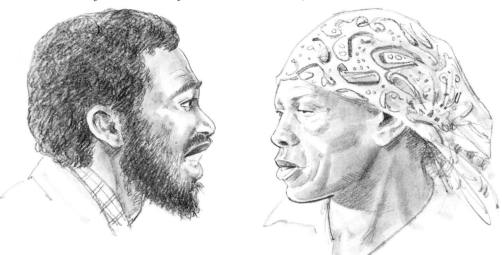

Bailey was the greatest person in my world. And the fact that he was my
brother, my only brother, and I had no sisters to share him with, was such
good fortune that it made me want to live a Christian life just to show God
that I was grateful. Where I was big, elbowy and grating, he was small, graceful and smooth. When I was described by our playmates as being dirt colour,
he was praised for his velvet-black skin. His hair fell down in black curls, and
my head was covered with black steel wool. And yet he loved me.

When our elders said unkind things about my features (my family was
handsome to a point of pain for me), Bailey would wink at me from across the
room, and I knew that it was a matter of time before he would take revenge.
He would allow the old ladies to finish wondering how on earth I came
about, then he would ask, in a voice like cooling bacon grease, 'Oh Mizeriz
Coleman, how is your son? I saw him the other day, and he looked sick
enough to die.'

Aghast, the ladies would ask, 'Die? From what? He ain't sick.'

And in a voice oilier than the one before, he'd answer with a straight face, 'From the uglies.'

I would hold my laugh, bite my tongue, grit my teeth and remove even the touch of a smile from my face. Later, behind the house by the black-walnut tree, we'd laugh and laugh and howl.

Bailey could count on very few punishments for his consistently out-rageous behaviour, for he was the pride of the Henderson/Johnson family.

His movements, as he was later to describe those of an acquaintance, were activated with oiled precision. He was also able to find more hours in the day than I thought existed. He finished chores, homework, read more books than I and played the group games on the side of the hill with the best of them. He could even pray out loud in church, and was apt at stealing pickles from the barrel that sat under the fruit counter and Uncle Willie's nose.

After our early chores were done, while Uncle Willie or Momma minded the Store, we were free to play the children's games as long as we stayed within yelling distance. Playing hide-and-seek, his voice was easily identified, singing, 'Last night, night before, twenty-four robbers at my door. Who all is hid? Ask me to let them in, hit 'em in the head with a rolling pin. Who all is hid?'. In follow the leader, naturally he was the one who created the most daring and interesting things to do.

Of all the needs a lonely child has, the one that must be satisfied, if there is going to be hope, is the unshaking need for an unshakable God. My pretty Black brother was my Kingdom Come.

For discussion

1 What are some of the qualities the writer most admired in her brother?
2 What are any of the qualities she felt she did not have as a child?
3 What does the last sentence mean?

*This is an extract from the magazine **Foxfire** and is one of a collection of stories which people have told about themselves when they have been interviewed by students from a local school. In this extract Lawton Brooks talks about his childhood.*

Me and my parents spent a lot of time together, because we were generally always around the farm. They were pretty strict — they *tried* to make a good man out of me! We had to go to church, and of a night time we always had family prayer. They wouldn't let us get in the bed without that. There's a whole lot of difference in the way I was raised and the way kids are raised now — the way I see it. You don't see much family prayer going on now.

One time me and a boy went by the store after school, and he got some cigars. There was a big old showcase sitting up there, and in one corner was a hole that you could get your hand through and there was a cigar box under it. We always stopped at the store to get us a piece of candy of an evening after school — get a great big piece for a penny. He says to me, 'Let's get us a cigar.'

I said, 'I ain't got no money.'

He said, 'I ain't, but I'm gonna just reach down there and get one apiece. Will you smoke one?'

I'd never smoked any, but I said, 'Yeah.' He reached down and got us one apiece. We stopped at a branch and lit those things and smoked a puff or two, and I began to get about half sick, and we smoked another round or two going up the road, and Lord, have mercy! I kept getting sicker and sicker, and I threw mine down, and drank some water out of a mudhole. When I did, I commenced throwing up. I got to the house and laid down on the porch. I wasn't able to go on in the house. When my daddy came home from the mill, he said, 'Son, what's the matter with you?'

I said, 'I'm sick, Poppy.' And he bent over me to see what was the matter with me and he smelled that cigar.

He said, 'You're been a'smoking.'

I told him, 'Yeah.' There wasn't no call to tell him not.

He said, 'Where did you get it?'

I said, 'Down at the store.'

And he asked me where I got the money, and I told him I didn't have no money. I said that boy got it. So he said, 'Let's me and you go to the store.'

Well, I wasn't able to go; I was about dead, but I had to go. I had to walk about a mile and a half down a hot river road, the sun just a'boiling down. Honestly, I was dragging; I'd never been as sick in my life, but my daddy made me go. He told me to tell the storekeeper just exactly what happened. Well, I had to tell him. I just told him that we got us a cigar, and that tickled him to death, 'cause I was so sick. I was so weak, I was just trembling all over. Poppy gave me the money and says, 'Now you pay him for it.'

The storekeeper wouldn't have it. He says, 'John, he's done learned his lesson. That boy had never done that before and he'll never do it again.' Sure enough, I didn't.

That other boy ran home, and his daddy whipped the dickens out of him, and made him go back to the store and pay for the cigar. And that broke us. We never did take nothing else. They tried to raise us children right back in them days.

For discussion

1 **Lawton Brooks says his parents were strict. Is there any evidence of this in the story?**
2 **What difference is there between Lawton's father and the other boy's father?**

BLACK BOY

Re-read the extract from Richard Wright's auto-biography *Black Boy* **in Unit 8, pp. 95–6.**

For discussion

1 Maya Angelou greatly admired her brother. Whom did Richard Wright greatly admire when he was a child? Whom did Lawton Brooks admire?

2 Richard had to prove that he was tough enough to fight back against the bullies in the street. Was there anything that Maya felt she had to prove? Or Lawton?

3 From what you have read in these three extracts, which one had the hardest time as a child? Which one seems to have been the happiest child?

Questions on the three extracts

Working on your own, re-read the three extracts (*Black Boy, Foxfire* **and** *I Know Why The Caged Bird Sings*) **and answer the questions below.**

Keep on re-reading the extracts until you decide on your answers.

Write out the numbers 1 to 10 underneath each other in your notebook and choose the *best* **answer for each question. Just write (a), (b) or (c).**

1 A word in the first paragraph of *Black Boy* means *noise*. The word is
   a) gauntly.
   b) baffled.
   c) clamour.

2 In Maya's eyes, the most amazing thing about her brother was that he
   a) loved her.
   b) was so much more handsome and graceful than she was.
   c) both a) *and* b).

3 In the last paragraph of Lawton's story, he says — 'And that broke us.' This means
   a) Lawton and his friend never spoke to each other again.
   b) Lawton and his friend never stole anything again.
   c) Lawton and his friend grew up to be good and honest.

4 A word in the third paragraph of *Black Boy* means *seriously*. The word is
   a) finally.
   b) vague.
   c) solemnly.

5 The word *chores* (in Maya Angelou's story) means
   a) jobs.
   b) games.
   c) prayers.

6 All three story-tellers have things in common. Which one of these do they *not* have in common?
   a) They are all American.
   b) They all had unhappy childhoods.
   c) They all had adventures.

7 Maya's and Richard's childhoods were similar in that both children were
   a) lonely.
   b) bullied.
   c) ugly.

8 Bailey was seldom punished because
   a) he never did anything wrong.
   b) the family were proud of him.
   c) he was so handsome.

9 Which of these did Bailey not do?
   a) Play truant from school.
   b) Read books.
   c) Play games.

10 Which of these were both Maya and Lawton expected to do?
   a) Pray.
   b) Play games.
   c) Do their homework.

11 Richard's mother and Lawton's father treat their children in the same way. They are both
   a) strict.
   b) cruel.
   c) careless.

12 Which of these statements is *not* true?
   a) All three writers wish they could be young again.
   b) All three writers remember their childhood very clearly.
   c) All three writers learned a lot when they were children.

13 Which writer seems to have had the worst father?
   a) Richard.
   b) Maya.
   c) Lawton.

14 Who seems to feel that children are not so well brought up
   as they used to be? Is it
   a) Richard?
   b) Maya?
   c) Lawton?

15 An autobiography is
   a) a person's life-story, written by that person.
   b) a person's life-story, written by someone else.
   c) any kind of story that is true.

Auto and other Prefixes

A *prefix* **is a group of letters used in front of a word to alter its meaning.**

For example, *autobiography* **uses the prefix** *auto.* **Auto is taken from a Greek word meaning** *by oneself,* **or** *by the same.*

So an autobiography is a person's life story written by that person.

The English language makes great use of many different prefixes.

1 The prefix *auto*

What word begins with the prefix *auto* and means
a)   working without any thought?
b)   a handwritten signature?
c)   driven by itself; a motor car?
d)   someone who rules a country on his own?
When you have worked out your answers, arrange them in the order in which you would find them in a dictionary. Then use a dictionary to check that you are right.

2 The prefix *un*

In the extract from Maya Angelou's autobiography, she writes in the last paragraph about a need that is *un*shaken and *un*shakable. The prefix *un* means *not.*
Make a list of ten words beginning with the prefix *un,* and then arrange them in the order in which you would find them in a dictionary.
Check their spelling and their meaning in a dictionary.

3 The prefix *ex*

To *exclude* someone means to 'leave them out of your company'. The prefix *ex* often means *out of. Exclude* means 'leave out of.'
What word begins with the prefix *ex* and means
a)   part of an engine through which gas or steam is passed out?
b)   a way out?
Check your answers in a dictionary.

4 The prefix *pre*

The word *prefix* itself begins with a prefix. *Pre* means *before.* So *prefix* means *placed before.*
What word begins with the prefix *pre* and means
a)   get ready?
b)   like better?
c)   already built; a small house that is built before it is delivered?
Check your answers in a dictionary.

5 Revision

Think of one word that means each of the following. All the words must begin with the prefix *auto, un, ex,* or *pre.*
a)   A pupil at school placed in charge of other pupils.
b)   An automatic pilot.
c)   To do with something that happened before history began.
d)   To stop something from happening.
e)   Not lucky.
f)   Cannot be stopped.
g)   To shout out.
h)   To look at something before other people do.
i)   To drive out, to stop someone from coming to school.
j)   To burst out with violence (like a bomb).
Check your answers in a dictionary.

Suggestions for improvisation and for writing

1 Interview a member of the class about their life so far, or about something interesting that they have done. Then write an account of the interview as if you are that person.

2 Choose a topic such as getting into trouble or nerve-racking moments, and interview members of the class getting them to tell their own experiences. Perhaps interview a member of your family or a neighbour. Write a report of one of the interviews.

3 Look at the illustrations on p. 157. Write the imaginary memoirs or part of the memoirs of one of the people (or of a group of people). Alternatively, bring in some pictures of your own.

Before writing:

Role-play: interview members of the class as if they are themselves the people you are going to write about. Ask them all kinds of questions to build up a full idea of the lives and characters of the people.
Improvisation: choose some stories from (2) and improvise them.

Suggestions for reading

A list of autobiographies and memoirs was given at the end of Unit 4. Here are some more suggestions:

David ATTENBOROUGH (editor)
My Favourite Stories of Exploration

A collection of travellers' tales, mostly written by the travellers themselves. Includes the story of a descent into an active volcano, a mountaineering story about the first successful ascent of Kangchenjunga, and an adventure of the real Robinson Crusoe (Alexander Selkirk) on his deserted island.

Aidan CHAMBERS (editor)
War at Sea

True stories, told by the seamen who fought in the Second World War. Includes tales of shipwreck, submarine fighting and the battle of the giant warships.

Richard HUMBLE
Marco Polo

Account of Polo's amazing travels to China and to the ends of the Earth. Well illustrated. Draws extensively on Polo's own account of his adventures.

Gillian AVERY (editor)
Unforgettable Journeys

Varied collection of personal experiences, including Leopold Mozart's account of a *Concert Tour*, C.S. Lewis and his journey *To School*, Laurie Lee's *The Choir Outing*, and Steven Runciman's *Children's Crusade*.

Francis CHICHESTER
The Lonely Sea and The Sky

The autobiography of the winner of the first solo sailing race across the Atlantic (1960), and the first man to sail without stopping on his own round the world (1966–7).

Roald DAHL
Boy — Tales of Childhood

Fascinating collection of memories of childhood. See especially the chapters entitled *The Headmaster, Fagging* and *Chocolate* — this last chapter tells how the idea was born for a very famous novel!

Suggestions for reading . . . continued

Alan C. JENKINS (editor)
Eye Witness

Unique collection of first-hand accounts of great adventures, including Charles Lindbergh (*Start of an Epic Flight*), Marco Polo (*In Xanadu did Kubla Khan*), and Edmund Hillary (*Room at the Top*).

Frank KNIGHT
Captain Cook and the Voyage of The Endeavour

Tells the story of Cook's travels using extracts from Cook's own journal, but the spelling and punctuation and sentence-structure are modernised to make the story more readable.

William MARCH (editor)
Company K

Collection of stories by soldiers of the First World War.

P.R. REID (editor)
My Favourite Escape Stories

First-hand accounts of escapes from The Tower of London, from American Civil War prisons, from transport ships, from Colditz Castle, and from Swanwick prisoner-of-war camp in England.

George SANDERLIN
First Around the World

Uses original source materials to tell the story of Magellan's voyage of 1519. Includes material taken from log-books, letters, memoirs and other contemporary reports.

Monica VINCENT
Girl Against the Jungle

The true story of a girl's struggle to survive when her plane crashes in the South American jungle. Her mother is killed, and the girl has to make her way on her own.